A Christmas Accident

And Other Stories

Annie Eliot Trumbull

[ZHINGOORA BOOKS]

This edition is published by
Zhingoora Books.

The Cover is Designed by Pallav Sethiya.

Contents

AT first the two yards were as much alike as the two houses, each house being the exact copy of the other. They were just two of those little red brick dwellings that one is always seeing side by side in the outskirts of a city, and looking as if the occupants must be alike too. But these two families were quite different. Mr. Gilton, who lived in one, was a pretty cross sort of man, and was quite well-to-do, as cross people sometimes are. He and his wife lived alone, and they did not have much going out and coming in, either. Mrs. Gilton would have liked more of it, but she had given up thinking about it, for her husband had said so many times that it was women's tomfoolery to want to have people, whom you weren't anything to and who weren't anything to you, ringing your doorbell all the time and bothering around in your dining-room,—which of course it was; and she would have believed it if a woman ever did believe anything a man says a great many times.

In the other house there were five children, and, as Mr. Gilton said, they made too large a family, and they ought to have gone somewhere else. Possibly they would have gone had it not been for the fence; but when Mr. Gilton put it up and Mr. Bilton told him it was three inches too far on his land, and Mr. Gilton said he could go to law about it, expressing the idea forcibly, Mr. Bilton was foolish enough to take his advice. The decision went against him, and a good deal of his money went with it, for it was a long, teasing lawsuit, and instead of being three inches of made ground it might have been three degrees of the Arctic Circle for the trouble there was in getting at it. So Mr. Bilton had to stay where he was.

It was then that the yards began to take on those little differences that soon grew to be very marked. Neither family would plant any vines because they would have been certain to heedlessly beautify the other side, and consequently the fence, in all its primitive boldness, stood out uncompromisingly, and the one or two little bits of trees grew carefully on the farther side of the enclosure so as not to be mixed up in the trouble at all. But Mr. Gilton's grass was cut smoothly by the man who made the fires, while Mr. Bilton only found a chance to cut his himself once in two weeks. Then, by and by, Mr. Gilton bought a red garden bench and put it under the tree that was nearest to the fence. No one ever went out and sat on it, to be sure, but to the Bilton children it represented the visible flush of prosperity. Particularly was Cora Cordelia wont to peer through the fence and gaze upon that red bench, thinking it a charming place in which to play house, ignorant of the fact that much of the red paint would have come off on her back. Cora Cordelia was the youngest of the five. All the rest had very simple names,—John, Walter, Fanny, and Susan,—but when it came to Cora Cordelia, luxuries were beginning to get very scarce in the Bilton family, and Mrs. Bilton felt that she must make up for it by being lavish, in one direction or another. She had wished to name Fanny, Cora, and Susan, Cordelia, but she had yielded to her husband, and called one after his mother and one after herself, and then gave both her favorite names to the youngest of all. Cora Cordelia was a pretty little girl, prettier even than both her names put together.

After the red bench came a quicksilver ball, that was put in the middle of the yard and reflected all the glory of its owner, albeit in a somewhat distorted form. This effort of human ingenuity filled the Bilton children with admiration bordering on awe; Cora Cordelia spent hours gazing at it, until called in and reproved by her mother for admiring so much things she could not afford to have. After this, she only admired it covertly.

Small distinctions like these barbed the arrows of contrast and comparison and kept the disadvantages of neighborhood ever present.

Then, it was a constant annoyance to have their surnames so much alike. Matters were made more unpleasant by mistakes of the butcher, the grocer, and so on,—Gilton, 79 Holmes Avenue, was so much like Bilton, 77 Holmes Avenue. Gilton changed his butcher every time he sent his dinner to Bilton; and though the mistakes were generally rectified, neither of the two families ever forgot the time the Biltons ate, positively ate, the Gilton dinner, under a misapprehension. Mrs. Bilton apologized, and Mrs. Gilton boldly told her husband that she was glad they'd had it, and she hoped they'd enjoyed it, which only made matters worse; and altogether it was a dark day, the only joy of it being that fearful one snatched by John, Walter, Susan, Fanny, and Cora Cordelia from the undoubted excellence of the roast.

Of course there was an assortment of minor difficulties. The smoke from the Biltons' kitchen blew in through the windows of the Giltons' sitting-room when the wind was in one direction, and, when it was in the other, many of the clothes from the Giltons' clothesline were blown into the Biltons' yard, and Fanny, Susan, or Cora Cordelia had to be sent out to pick them up and drop them over the fence again, which Mrs. Bilton said was very wearing, as of course it must have been. Things like this were always happening, but matters reached a climax when it came to the dog. It wasn't a large dog, but it was a tiresome one. It got up early in the morning and barked. Now we all know that early rising is a good thing and honorable among all men, but it is something that ought to be done quietly, out of regard to the weaker vessels; and a dog that barks between five and seven in the morning, continuously, certainly ought to be suppressed, even if it be necessary to use force. Everybody agreed with the Biltons about that,—everybody except the Giltons themselves, who, by some one of nature's freaks, didn't mind it. Mrs. Bilton often said she wished Mrs. Gilton could be a light sleeper for a week and see what it was like. So, too, everybody thought that Mr. Bilton had right on his side when he complained that this same dog came into his yard, being apparently indifferent to any coolness between the estate owners, and ran over a bed of geraniums and one thing and another, that was the small Bilton offset to the Gilton bench and ball. But when one morning, for the first time, that dog remained quiet and restful, and was found cold and poisoned, and Mr. Gilton was loud in his accusations of the Bilton boys and their father, public opinion wavered for a moment. After that accident, no member of either family spoke to any member of the other. That was the way matters stood the day before Christmas.

It was snowing hard, and the afternoon grew dark rapidly, and the whirling flakes pursued a blinding career. In spite of that, everybody was out doing the last thing. Mrs. Gilton was not, to be sure. Of course they would have a big dinner, but even that was all arranged for, although the turkey hadn't come and her husband was going to stop and see about it on his way home. She shuddered as the possibility of its having gone to the Biltons occurred to her. But she didn't believe it had,—they hadn't the same butcher any longer. Meanwhile there was so little to do. It was too dark to read or sew, and she sat idly at the window looking out at the passers and the driving snow. Everybody else was in a hurry. She wished she, too, had occasion to hasten down for a last purchase, or to light the lamp in order to finish a last bit of dainty sewing, as she used to do when she was a girl. She seemed to have so few friends now with whom she exchanged Christmas greetings. Was it then only for children and youth, this Christmas cheer? And must she necessarily have left it behind her with her girlhood? No, she knew better than that. She felt that there was a deeper significance in the Christmas-tide than can come home to the hearts of children and unthoughtfulness, and yet it had grown to be so painfully like other days,—an occasion for a little bigger dinner, that was about all. With an unconscious sigh she looked across to the Bilton house. Plenty of people over there to make merry. Five stockings to hang up. She wished she might have sent something in. To be sure, there was the dog, but that was some time ago. Very likely the dog would have been dead now, anyhow. She felt, herself, that this logic was not irrefutable, but she wished she could have sent some paper parcels just the same. So strong had this impulse been that she had said to her husband somewhat timidly that morning,—

"There are a good many of those Bilton children to get presents for."

"More fools they that get 'em presents, then," he had pleasantly replied.

"I don't suppose he has much to buy them with," she continued.

"He had enough to buy poison for my dog," exclaimed her husband, giving his newspaper an angry shake.

"I'd almost like to send them in some cheap little toys."

"Well, as long as you don't quite like to, it won't do any harm," he said with some violence, laying down his newspaper, and looking at her in a manner not to be misunderstood. "But you see that the liking doesn't get any farther."

"It's Christmas, you know," said his plucky wife.

"Oh, no, I don't know it!" he replied gruffly. "I haven't fallen over forty children a minute in the street with their ridiculous parcels, and I haven't had women drop brown-paper bundles that come undone all over me when they crowd into the horse car, and I haven't found it impossible to get to the shirt-collar counter on account of Christmas novelties! Oh, no, I didn't know it was Christmas!"

After that there was really not much to be said, for we all know Christmas is dreadfully annoying, and the last thing a man in this sort of temper wants to hear about is peace and good will.

Notwithstanding the fact that Mrs. Gilton looked over to her neighbors' with an envious feeling this dark afternoon, their Christmas cheer was not so abounding as it had been in more prosperous times. There was not very much money to be spent this year, and they were obliged to give up something. Mr. and Mrs. Bilton had decided that it should be the Christmas dinner; they would have a simple luncheon, and let all the money that could be spared go for the stockings. Each child had its own sum to invest for others, and there was still a small amount for the older members of the family. That it was a small amount Mrs. Bilton felt strongly, as she went from shop to shop. But when she reached home again she was somewhat encouraged; there was such an air of joyous expectation in the house, and her purchases looked larger now that they were away from the glittering counters. Then each of the five children came to her separately and confided to her the nothing less than wonderful results of judicious bargaining which had enabled them to buy useful and beautiful presents for each of the others out of the sums intrusted to their care, ranging in amount from the two dollars of John to the fifty cents of Cora Cordelia. She felt sure that there were further secrets yet; secrets attended by brown paper and string, which she had taken the greatest care for the last two weeks not heedlessly to expose,—

riddles of which the solution lay perilously near her eyes, which would be revealed to her astonished gaze the next morning.

She had reason to believe that even Cora Cordelia was making something for her, and though it was difficult for her to ignore the fact that it was a knit washcloth, she had hitherto avoided absolute certainty on the subject. So that altogether it was a pretty cheerful afternoon at the Biltons'.

Meanwhile, down in the main street of the city it was a confusing scene. It was darker there than where the streets were more open; and although there were several daring spirits of that adventurous turn of mind which leads people into byways of discovery, who asserted that the street lamps were lighted, it was not generally believed. The snow was blowing down and up and across, and getting more and more unmanageable under the feet of foot passengers every moment. It was cold and windy and blinding and crowded, and a good many other disconcerting things, all of which Mr. Gilton felt the full force of as he stood on the corner where he had just bought his turkey. It was a fine turkey, and had been a good bargain, and though he had to carry it home himself, there was nothing derogatory in that. If it had been anybody else he would have been thrilled with a glow of satisfaction, but Mr. Gilton was long past glows of satisfaction—it was years since he had permitted himself to have such things.

"Jour—our—nal! fi-i-i-ve cents!" screamed an intermittent newsboy in his ear.

"Get out!" replied Mr. Gilton, the uncompromising nature of his language being intensified by the fact that he jumped nearly two feet from the suddenness of the newsboy's attack. Even the newsboy, inured to the short words of an unfriendly world, and usually quite indifferent thereto, was impressed by the asperity of the suggestion and moved somewhat hastily on. Possibly his cold, wet little existence had been rendered morbidly susceptible by the general good feeling of the hour, one lady having even spontaneously given him five cents.

After this exchange of amenities Mr. Gilton stepped into his horse car. It was crowded, of course, as horse cars that are small and run once in half an hour are apt to be, and he had to stand up, and the turkey legs stuck out of the brown paper in a very conspicuous way. If Mr. Gilton had been anybody else he would have been chaffed about his turkey, because to make up for the conveniences that the horse car line did not furnish the public, the large-hearted public furnished the horse car line with an unusual amount of friendliness. There was almost always something going on in these horse cars. Their social privileges were quite a feature. To-night they were in unusual force on account of the season. But nobody said anything to Mr. Gilton. Only when he jerked the bell and stepped off, one stout man with his overcoat collar turned up to his ears said, without turning his head:—

"I supposed of course he was going to give the turkey to the conductor."

Everybody laughed in that end of the car except one small old lady in the corner, who was a stranger and visiting, and who was left with the impression that the gentleman who got off must be a very kind man. It was darker and blowier and snowier than when he had left the corner, and Mr. Gilton floundered through the unbroken drifts up the little path to the door with increasing grudges in his heart against the difficulties of Christmas. The lock was off, and he went in slamming the door after him. There was no light in the hall, and he murmured loudly against the inconvenience.

"Confound it!" he said, "why didn't they light the gas? I'm not one of those confounded Biltons; I can afford to pay for what I don't get;" and, without pausing to take off his hat and coat, he strode to the sitting-room door and flung it open. That was an awful moment. The sudden change from the cold and darkness almost blinded him, and confirmed the impression that he was the victim of an illusion. The sound of many voices, and then the hush of sudden consternation, was in his ears. There was a lamp and there was a fire, and there between them sat Mr. Bilton on one side and Mrs. Bilton on the other, and round about, in various unconventional attitudes, sat four Bilton children. And there in the very midst of them, in his heavy overcoat, with snow melting on his hat, his beard, and his shoulders, stood Mr. Gilton. The unexpected scene, the amazed faces gazing into his, rendered him speechless; he wondered vaguely if he were losing his reason. Then, in a flush of enlightenment, he realized what had happened; thanks to the storm outside, he had come into the wrong house. Naturally his first impulse was towards flight, but as his bewildered gaze slipped about the room it fell upon five stockings hung against the mantelpiece, and stayed there fascinated. Five foolish, limp, expressionless stockings,—it was long since he had seen such an unreasonable spectacle. Then he recollected himself and looked around him. Perhaps even then, if he had made a dash for the door, he might have escaped and matters have been none the worse. But in that instant of hesitation caused by the sudden sight of those five stockings something dreadful occurred. It must be premised that Cora Cordelia did not know Mr. Gilton very well by sight, being in the first place small and not noticing, and in the second, filled with an unreasoning fear that caused her to flee whenever she had seen him approach. This is the only excuse for what she did; for while her mother was feebly murmuring, as if in extenuation, "We thought it was John coming in," Cora Cordelia clasped her hands in delirious delight, and cried aloud, "It's Santa Claus! Oh, it's Santa Claus!" Could anything more awful happen to a cross man, a very cross man, than to be taken for Santa Claus!

Mr. Gilton looked at Cora Cordelia, and wondered why she had not been slaughtered in her cradle.

"And," exclaimed Susan Bilton, with sudden communicative fervor, "he has come and brought us a turkey for to-morrow's dinner!"

The truth was that Susan had been coming to the age that is sceptical about Santa Claus, but she could not resist this sudden appearance.

No one could appreciate the nonsense of the whole situation better than Mr. Gilton; and yet, strangely enough, together with his annoyance was mingled a touch of the strange feeling that had dawned upon him first when he saw the stockings. To be sure, it only added to his annoyance, but it was there. By this time—it was really a very short time—Mrs. Bilton had recovered herself and risen, and Mr. Bilton had risen too.

"Hush, children; it is not Santa Claus," she said, "it is Mr. Gilton. We are glad to see you, Mr. Gilton;" and she held out her hand to him. "Won't you sit down?" She felt that he had come in the Christmas spirit, and she was anxious to meet him half-way.

"Yes," said her husband, coming forward, and instantly taking his cue from his wife,—for he was really a very nice man,—"we are very glad." To be sure, in his manner there was a certain stiffness, for a man cannot always change completely in a moment, as a woman can; but Mr. Gilton was too perplexed to notice this. In the incomprehensible way that one's mind has of clinging to unimportant things at great crises, while he was fuming with rage and bothered with this strange feeling which was not precisely rage, he was wondering how in the world he was going to sit down with that ridiculous turkey, with its ridiculous legs, in his arms, and not look more absurd than he did now. In this moment of absentmindedness he had mechanically taken Mrs. Bilton's hand and shaken it, and after that of course there was nothing to do except to shake Mr. Bilton's. Then he began to know it was all up. He had not spoken yet, but now he made a frantic effort to save what might be left besides honor. "I came—" he began, "I came—came to your house—" There he paused a moment, and that unlucky child with that tendency to be possessed by one idea, which is characteristic of small and trivial minds, and for which she should have been shaken, burst in with, "And did the reindeer bring you, and are they outside?"

He almost groaned, so overwhelmed was he by this new idiocy. Reindeer! If those overworked, struggling car-horses could have heard that! Then Mrs. Bilton, pitying his evident confusion, came to his assistance.

"Don't mind the children, Mr. Gilton," she said, her cheeks flushing, and looking very pretty with the excitement of the unusual circumstances, "we are glad you came, however you made your way here. I think we may thank Christmas Eve for it. Now do take off your overcoat and sit down."

Oh, mispraised woman's tact! What complications you may produce! That finished it, of course. He sat down. In those few moments that strange feeling had grown marvellously stronger. It seemed to be made up of the most diverse elements,—a mixture of green wreaths and his own childhood, and his mother, and a top he had not thought of for years, and the wide fireplace at home, and a stable with a child in it, and a picture, in a book he used to read, of a lot of angels in the sky, one particular one in the middle, and underneath it some words—what were the words? He'd forgotten they had anything to do with Christmas, anyway.

"But you *did* bring us the turkey, didn't you?" said Cora Cordelia, helping her mother on.

To do the child justice,—for even Cora Cordelia has a right to demand justice,—her manners were corrupted by Christmas expectancy.

"Cora Cordelia, I'm ashamed of you," said Mrs. Bilton.

"Yes," said Mr. Gilton, the words wrung from his lips, while beads stood on his forehead,—"yes, I brought you the turkey."

"Did you really?" exclaimed Mrs. Bilton, who thought he had all the time. "That was very kind of you."

"Will you please take it—take it away?" he said, with that wish to have something over which we associate with the dentist. So Mrs. Bilton took the turkey and thanked him, and gave it to Fanny, who carried it out to the kitchen, and Mr. Gilton gave one last look at its legs as it went through the door, feeling that now he must wake up from this nightmare. But things only went farther and became more incredible and upsetting, only that, strangely enough, that feeling of horror began to wear off, and that singular strain of association with all sorts of Christmas things to grow stronger. He himself could hardly believe that it was no worse, when he found himself seated by the littered table, with Mrs. Bilton near and Mr. Bilton over by the fire again, listening to first one and then the other, and occasionally letting fall a word himself, his conversational powers seeming to thaw out along with the snow on his greatcoat. These words themselves were a surprise to him. He was quite sure that he started them with a creditable gruffness, but the Christmas air mellowed them in a highly unsatisfactory fashion, so that they fell on his own ears quite otherwise than as he had meant they should sound. Moreover the general tenor of the conversation was exceedingly perplexing. It was all about how fine it was of him to come this evening, and how they had often regretted the hard feeling, and how things always did get exaggerated. Of course he would not have believed a word of it, if he had been able to get any grip on the situation, but he wasn't, and he just went on assenting to it all as if it were true. There came a time when Mr. Bilton cleared his throat, hesitated a moment, and then said boldly,—

"I think I ought to tell you, Mr. Gilton, that I had nothing whatever to do with the death of your dog." Mr. Gilton felt the ground slipping away from under his very feet. That dog had been his piece of resistance, as it were. "I wouldn't have poisoned him," went on Mr. Bilton, "for a hundred dollars. But," he added, with a queer little smile, "I wasn't going to tell you so, you know."

"Of course you wasn't," exclaimed Mr. Gilton, hurriedly, with a touch of that unholy excitement that a lapse from grammar imparts.

"We wouldn't any of us," asserted Walter.

"No," said Susan, Fanny, and Cora Cordelia.

Then it came out that the whole family had rather admired the dog than otherwise. It was here that John did really come in, his entrance sounding very much as had Mr. Gilton's. He nearly fell over when he saw the visitor, but he had time to pull himself together, for Cora Cordelia had snatched that moment for showing Mr. Gilton her gifts for the family, and he was bound hand and foot with helplessness. Then they all came and showed him their gifts. While he examined them Mr. and Mrs. Bilton carefully averted their eyes and gazed hard at the opposite wall, while Cora Cordelia urged him, in stage whispers, not to let them suspect. It was pitiable the state to which he was reduced. Of course resisting this Christmas enthusiasm was out of the question. To be sure it came over him once with startling force, as she showed him a toy water-wheel, that went by sand,—which she had purchased for her father at a phenomenally low rate because the wheel could not be made to go,—that Cora Cordelia was the very child that he had fallen over as she came hastening out of a toy-shop with a queerly shaped bundle, the day before, and so been further imbittered towards Christmas. Susan had purchased a cup and ball for her mother, and as she went out of the room for a moment, insisted upon Mr. Gilton's trying to do it and see what fun it was. If Mr. Gilton lives to be a hundred he will never forget the mingled feelings with which he awkwardly tried to get that senseless ball into that idiotic cup. At last he stood up to go—it was after six o'clock—and they went with him to the door, and wished him Merry Christmas, and sent Merry Christmas to Mrs. Gilton, and said good-night several times, and he stumbled on through the snow, this time towards his own door. It had stopped snowing as suddenly and quietly as it had begun, and the stars had come out. He gazed up at them,—something he very rarely did. They seemed a part of Christmas. Just before he turned in at his own gate, he looked back at the Bilton house and shook his fist at it, but the expression on his face was such that the very same newsboy who had accosted him earlier failed utterly to recognize him and was emboldened to offer him a paper. He too was pushing his way home with two papers left, in a somewhat dispirited way.

"I'll take 'em both," said this singular customer. "Here's a quarter—never mind the change. It's Christmas Eve, I believe—" and this when he knew perfectly well that a copy of that very same journal was waiting for him on his table. The boy looked at his quarter and looked again at his customer, and recognized him, and made up his mind to buy a couple of hot sausages on the corner, and went on his way feeling that there was a new heaven and a new earth. Mrs. Gilton was standing at the parlor window, peering out anxiously as he came up the path. She was in the hall as he entered.

"Why, Reuben," she said, "I was afraid something had happened."

Goodness gracious! As if something hadn't happened! He turned away to hang up his overcoat and tried to speak crossly.

"Well," he said, "I've lost my turkey. That's happened."

"Never mind," said Mrs. Gilton, quickly; "the other one came later, the first one, you know—so—so the Biltons didn't get it this time."

"They got the second one, though," said Reuben, hanging up his hat.

"Oh, dear, did they!" said Mrs. Gilton. Then she went on, "Well, I don't care if they did, so there! I guess they need it for their Christmas dinner."

"No, they don't," said Reuben, turning around and facing her, "because they are going to eat part of ours. They are coming in to-morrow to have dinner with us,—every one of them!" he asserted more loudly, on account of the expression on his wife's face. "Bilton, and his wife, and all the five children, down to Cora Cordelia! So we'll have to have something for them to eat."

If Mr. Gilton will never forget the cup and ball, Mrs. Gilton will never forget that moment. She went all over it in her mind whether she could manage him herself to-night, or whether to send Bridget right away then for the doctor, and if she hadn't better say a policeman too, and whether he could be kept for the future in a private house, or would have to be confined in an asylum. She was inclining towards the asylum when he, who was going into the sitting-room before her, turned round and laughed an odd little laugh. She began to think then that a private house would do.

The next day they all dined together, which proved that it was not all a Christmas Eve illusion. There is a report in the neighborhood that the fence between the houses is to be taken down to make room for a tennis court for the Bilton children, but of course this may not be true. It would have to be done in the summer, and if the effect of Christmas could be depended upon to last into the summer this would be a very different sort of world.

After—the Deluge

THE sombre tints of Grayhead were slightly suffused by a pink light sifting from the west through the clear air. The yachts in the harbor lay idly beneath the mellow influences of the passing of the summer day,—idly as only sailboats can lie, a bit of loose sail or cordage now and then flapping inconsistently in a breath of wind, which seemed to come out of the west for no other purpose, and to retire into the east afterward, its whole duty done. On board, men were moving about, hanging lanterns, making taut here, setting free there, all with an air of utter peace and repose such as is found only on placid waterways beneath a setting sun. Occasionally an oar dipped in the still water, a hint of action, modified, softened into repose. Along one of the quaint streets of the irregular town, winding where it would, climbing where it climbed, hurried an angular figure,—that of a woman of about fifty years, whose tense expression suggested an unrest at variance with the keen calmness of that of the other faces about the streets and doorways. Not that it was feverish in its intensity; rather, it was an expression of resolution, undeviating and persistent, but not sure of sympathy or support.

"They've gone down yonder, t'other side of the wharf, Mis' Pember," said a middle-aged sea captain, whose interest in his kind had not been obliterated by the forced loneliness of northern voyages.

The woman paused and glanced doubtfully down one of the byways that led between small, weather-beaten houses and around disconcerting abutments to the water, and then forward, straight along the way she had been travelling, which led out of the town.]

"I'd rather fixed on their going down Point-ways this evening," she said.

"Well, they ain't," rejoined Captain Phippeny, with that absence of mere rhetoric characteristic of people whose solid work is done otherwise than by speech.

Mrs. Pember nodded, at once in acknowledgment and farewell, and, turning about, followed the path he had indicated, her gait acquiring a certain precipitancy as she went down the rough, stony slope. At the foot of the descent she paused again, and looked to the right and left. Captain Phippeny was watching her from his vantage ground above. His figure was one unmistakably of the seaboard. His trousers were of a singular cut, probably after a pattern evolved in all its originality by Mrs. Phippeny, her active imagination working towards practical effect. In addition, he wore a yellow flannel shirt ribbed with purple, which would hopelessly have jaundiced a rose-leaf complexion, but which, having exhausted its malignancy without producing any particular effect, ended by gently harmonizing with the captain's sandy hair, reddish beard, and tanned skin. His mouth was like a badly made buttonhole, which gaped a little when he smiled. He had a nose like a parrot's beak, and his eyes were blue, kindly, and wise in their straightforwardness. When he would render his costume absolutely *de rigueur*, he wore a leathern jacket with manifold pockets, from one to another of which trailed a gold watch-chain with a dangling horseshoe charm.

"I wonder the old woman don't take a dog with her and trace 'em out, she spends so much time on the hunt," he said to himself. "I declare for't, it's a sing'lar thing the way she everlastin' does get onto them 'prentices; ain't old enough to talk about settin' sail by themselves."

His quid of tobacco again resumed its claim to his undivided attention, and he leaned back against the fence and waited as idly as the drooping sails for a breath of something stirring. By and by it appeared in the shape of another old sailor, between whom and himself there was the likeness of two peas, save for a slight discrepancy of feature useful for purposes of identification.

"You told her where they'd gone, I reckon," he remarked, with a slight chuckle, as he too leaned up against the fence and looked out over the harbor.

"Yes, I did," replied Captain Phippeny. "I didn't have no call to tell her a lie."

"Kinder hard on the young uns," observed the new-comer.

"They ain't ever anythin' as hard on the young uns as on the old uns," asserted Captain Phippeny, "because—well, because they're *young*, I guess. That's Chivy's yacht that came in just at sundown, ain't it?"

"Yare. They say she's seen dirty weather since she was here last."

"Has? Well, you can't stay in harbor allers, and git your livin' at the same time. She's got toler'ble good men to handle her."

There was a pause. The soft twilight was battening down the hatches of the day, to drop into the parlance of the locality.

"Well, I do suppose old Pember warn't an easy shipmate, blow or no blow," observed Captain Smart. He was a small, keen-eyed, quickly moving old man, seasoned with salt.

"I reckon he warn't. And she thinks she can keep that girl of hers out of the same kind of discipline that she had to take,—that's the truth of it."

"Cur'ous, ain't it?" ruminated Captain Smart. "A woman's bound to take it one way or 'nother; there seems to be more sorts of belayin' pins to knock 'em over with than they, any on 'em, kinder cal'late on at first."

"So there be," assented Captain Phippeny.

Near the water, with its fading, rose-colored reflections, not so far from the anchored vessels but they might, had they chosen, have spoken across to those on board, the monotonous, austere, and yet vaguely soft gray of the old town rising behind them against the melting sky, sat Mellony Pember and Ira Baldwin.

"If you'd only make up your mind, Mellony," urged the young man.

"I can't, Ira; don't ask me." The young girl's face, which was delicate in outline, was troubled, and the sensitive curves of her lips trembled. The faded blue of her dress harmonized with the soft tones of the scene; her hat lay beside her, an uncurled, articulated ostrich feather standing up in it like an exclamation point of brilliant red.

The young man pulled his hat over his eyes and looked over to the nearest boat. Mellony glanced at him timidly.

"You see, I'm all she's got," she said.

"I ain't goin' to take you away from her, unless you want to go," he replied, without looking at her.

"She thinks I'll be happier if I don't—if I don't marry."

"Happier!"—he paused in scorn—"and she badgerin' you all the time if you take a walk with me, and watchin' us as if we were thieves! You ain't happy now, are you?"

"No." Mellony's eyes filled, and a sigh caught and became almost a sob.

"Well, I wish she'd give me a try at makin' you happy, that's all." His would-be sulkiness softened into a tender sense of injury. Mellony twisted her hands together, and looked over beyond the vessels to the long, narrow neck of land with its clustering houses, beyond which again, unseen, were booming the waves of the Atlantic.

"Oh, if I only knew what to do!" she exclaimed,—"if I only knew what to do!"

"I'll tell you what to do, Mellony," he began.

"There's ma, now," she interrupted.

Ira turned quickly and looked over his shoulder. Across the uneven ground, straight towards them, came the figure of Mrs.

Pember. The tenseness of her expression had further yielded to resolution, which had in turn taken on a stolidity which declared itself unassailable. No one of the three spoke as she seated herself on a bit of timber near them, and, folding her hands, waited with the immobility and the apparent impartiality of Fate itself. At last Mellony spoke, for of the three she was the most acutely sensitive to the situation, and the least capable of enduring it silently.

"Which way did you come, ma?" she asked.

"I come down Rosaly's Lane," Mrs. Pember answered. "I met Cap'n Phippeny, and he told me you was down here.""I'm obligated to Cap'n Phippeny," observed Ira, bitterly.

"I dono as he's partickler to have you," remarked Mrs. Pember, imperturbably.

There was another silence. Mrs. Pember's voice had a marked sweetness when she spoke to her daughter, which it lost entirely when she addressed her daughter's companion, but always it was penetrated by the timbre of a certain inflexibility.

The shadows grew deeper on the water, the glow-worms of lanterns glimmered more sharply, and the softness of the night grew more palpable.

"I guess I may as well go back, ma," said Mellony, rising.

"I was wonderin' when you cal'lated on going," remarked her mother, as she rose too, more slowly and stiffly, and straightened her decent black bonnet.

"I suppose you was afraid Mellony wouldn't get back safe without you came after her," broke out Ira.

"I guess I can look after Mellony better than anybody else can, and I count on doing it, and doing it right along," she replied.

"Come, ma," said Mellony, impatiently; but she waited a moment and let her mother pass her, while she looked back at Ira, who stood, angry and helpless, kicking at the rusted timbers.

"Are you coming, too, Ira?" she asked in a low voice.

"No," he exclaimed, "I ain't coming! I don't want to go along back with your mother and you, as if we weren't old enough to be out by ourselves. I might as well be handcuffed, and so might you! If you'll come round with me the way we came, and let her go the way she came, I'll go with you fast enough."

Mellony's eyes grew wet again, as she looked from him to her mother, and again at him. Mrs. Pember had paused, also, and stood a little in advance of them. Her stolidity showed no anxiety; she was too sure of the result.

"No,"—Mellony's lips framed the words with an accustomed but grievous patience,—"I can't to-night, Ira; I must go with ma."

"It's to-night that'll be the last chance there'll be, maybe," he muttered, as he flung himself off in the other direction.

The two women walked together up the rough ascent, and turned into Rosaly's Lane. Mellony walked wearily, her eyes down, the red feather, in its uncurled, unlovely assertiveness, looking more like the oriflamme of a forlorn hope than ever. But Mrs. Pember held herself erect, and as if she were obliged carefully to repress what might have been the signs of an ill-judged triumph.

Ira prolonged his walk beyond the limits of the little gray town, goaded by the irritating pricks of resentment. He would bear it no longer, so he told himself. Mellony could take him or leave him. He would be a laughing-stock not another week, not another day. If Mellony would not assert herself against her tyrannical old mother, he would go away and leave her! And then he paused, as he had paused so often in the flood of his anger, faced by the realization that this was just what Mrs. Pember wanted, just what would satisfy her, what she had been waiting for,—that he should go away and leave Mellony alone. It was an exasperating dilemma, his abdication and her triumph, or his uncertainty and her anxiety.

Mellony and her mother passed Captain Phippeny and Captain Smart, who still stood talking in the summer evening, the fence continuing to supply all the support their stalwart frames needed in this their hour of ease. Captain Smart nudged Captain Phippeny as the two figures turned the corner of Rosaly's Lane.

"So you found 'em, Mis' Pember," remarked Captain Phippeny. He spoke to the mother, but he looked, not without sympathy at the daughter.

"Yes, I found 'em."

"You reckoned on fetchin' only one of 'em home, I take it," said Captain Smart.

"I ain't responsible but for one of 'em," replied Mrs. Pember with some grimness, but with her eyes averted from Mellony's crimsoning face.

"Come, ma," said Mellony again, and they passed on.

"Mis' Pember is likely enough lookin' woman herself," observed Captain Smart; "it's kind of cur'ous she should be so set agen marryin,' just as marryin'."

"'Tis so," assented Captain Phippeny, thoughtfully, looking after the two women.

Without speaking, Mellony and her mother entered the little house where they lived, and the young girl sank down in the stiff, high-backed rocker, with its thin calico-covered cushion tied with red braid, that stood by the window. Outside, the summer night buzzed and hummed, and breathed sweet odors. Mrs. Pember moved about the room, slightly altering its arrangements, now and then looking at her daughter half furtively, as if waiting for her to speak; but Mellony's head was not turned from the open window, and she was utterly silent. At last this immobility had a sympathetic effect upon the mother, and she seated herself not far from the girl, her hands, with their prominent knuckles and shrunken flesh, folded in unaccustomed idleness, and waited, while in the room dusk grew to dark. To Mellony the hour was filled with suggestions that emphasized and defined her misery. In her not turbulent or passionate nature, the acme of its capacity for emotional suffering had been reached. Hitherto this suffering had been of the perplexed, patient, submissive kind; to-night, the beauty of the softly descending gloom, the gentle freedom of the placid harbor, the revolt of her usually yielding lover, deepened it into something more acute.

"Mellony," said her mother, with a touch of that timidity which appeared only in her speech with her daughter, "did you count on going over to the Neck to-morrow, as you promised?"

"I'll never count on doing anything again," said Mellony, in a voice she tried to make cold and even, but which vibrated notwithstanding,—"never, so long as I live. I'll never think, or plan, or—or speak, if I can help it—of what I mean to do. I'll never do anything but just work and shut my eyes and—and live, if I've got to!" Her voice broke, and she turned her head away from the open window and looked straight before her into the shadowed room. Her mother moved uneasily, and her knotted hands grasped the arms of the stiff chair in which she sat.

"Mellony," she said again, "you've no call to talk so."

"I've no call to talk at all. I've no place anywhere. I'm not anybody. I haven't any life of my own." The keen brutality of the thoughtlessness of youth, and its ignoring of all claims but those of its own happiness, came oddly from the lips of submissive Mellony. Mrs. Pember quivered under it.

"You know you're my girl, Mellony," she answered gently. "You're all I've got."

"Yes," the other answered indifferently, "that's all I am,—Mellony Pember, Mrs. Pember's girl,—just that."

"Ain't that enough? Ain't that something to be,—all I plan for and work for? Ain't that enough for a girl to be?"

Mellony turned her eyes from emptiness, and fixed them upon her mother's face, dimly outlined in the vagueness.

"Is that all you've been," she asked, "just somebody's daughter?"

It was as if a heavy weight fell from her lips and settled upon her mother's heart. There was a silence. Mellony's eyes, though she could not see them, seemed to Mrs. Pember to demand an answer in an imperative fashion unlike their usual mildness.

"It's because I've been,—it's because I'd save you from what I have been that I—do as I do. You know that," she said.

"I don't want to be saved," returned the other, quickly and sharply.

The older woman was faced by a situation she had never dreamed of,—a demand to be allowed to suffer! The guardian had not expected this from her carefully shielded charge.

"I want you to have a happy life," she added.

"A happy life!" flashed the girl. "And you're keeping me from any life at all! That's what I want,—life, my own life, not what anybody else gives me of theirs. Why shouldn't I have what they have, even if it's bad now and then? Don't save me in spite of myself! Nobody likes to be saved in spite of themselves."

It was a long speech for Mellony. A large moon had risen, and from the low horizon sent golden shafts of light almost into the room; it was as if the placidity of the night were suddenly penetrated by something more glowing. Mellony stood looking down at her mother, like a judge. Mrs. Pember gazed at her steadily.

"I'm going to save you, Mellony," she said, her indomitable will making her voice harsher than it had been, "whether you want to be saved or not. I'm not going to have you marry, and be sworn at and cuffed." Mellony moved to protest, but her strength was futility beside her mother's at a time like this. "I'm not going to have you slave and grub, and get blows for your pains. I'm going to follow you about and set wherever you be, whenever you go off with Ira Baldwin, if that'll stop it; and if that won't, I'll try some other way,—I know other ways. I'm not going to have you marry! I'm going to have you stay along with me!"

With a slight gesture of despair, Mellony turned away. The flash had burned itself out. The stronger nature had reasserted itself. Silently, feeling her helplessness, frightened at her own rebellion now that it was over, she went out of the room to her own smaller one, and closed the door.

Mrs. Pember sat silent in her turn, reviewing her daughter's resentment, but the matter admitted no modifications in her mind; her duty was clear, and her determination had been taken long ago. Neither did she fear anything like persistent opposition; she knew her daughter's submissive nature well.

Brought up in a country village, an earnest and somewhat apprehensive member of the church, Mrs. Pember had married the captain early in life, under what she had since grown to consider a systematic illusion conceived and maintained by the Evil One, but which was, perhaps, more logically due to the disconcerting good looks and decorously restrained impetuosity of Captain Pember himself. Possibly he had been the victim of an illusion too, not believing that austerity of principle could exist with such bright eyes and red cheeks as charmed him in the country girl. At least, he never hesitated subsequently, not only to imply, but to state baldly, a sense of the existence of injury. Captain Phippeny was one of those sailors whom the change of scene, the wide knowledge of men and of things, the hardships and dangers of a sea life, broaden and render tolerant and somewhat wise. Pember had been brutalized by these same things.

The inhabitants of Grayhead were distinguished by the breadth and suggestiveness of their profanity, and Captain Pember had been a past master of the accomplishment. Praise from Sir Hubert Stanley could have been no more discriminating than the local acknowledgment of his proficiency in this line. No wonder Mrs. Pember looked back at the ten years of her married life with a shudder. With the rigid training of her somewhat dogmatic communion still potent, she listened in a horrified expectancy, rather actual than figurative, for the heavens to strike or the earth to swallow up her nonchalant husband. Nor was this all. The weakness for grog, unfortunately supposed to be inherent in a nautical existence, was carried by Captain Pember to an extent inconsiderate even in the eyes of a seafaring public; and when, under its genial influence, he knocked his wife down and tormented Mellony, the opinion of this same public declared itself on the side of the victims with a unanimity which is not always to be counted upon in such cases.

In fact, her married life had, as it were, formalized many hitherto somewhat vague details of Mrs. Pember's conception of the place of future punishment; and when her husband died in an appropriate and indecorous fashion as the result of a brawl, he continued to mitigate the relief of the event by leaving in his wife's heart a haunting fear, begotten of New England conscientiousness, that perhaps she ought not to be so unmistakably glad of it. It was thus that, with Mellony's growth from childhood to womanhood, the burning regret for her former unmarried state, whose difficulties had been mainly theological, had become a no less burning resolve that her child should never suffer as she had suffered, but should be guarded from matrimony as from death. That she failed to distinguish between individuals, that she failed to see that young Baldwin was destitute of those traits which her sharpened vision would now have detected in Pember's youth, was both the fault of her perceptive qualities and the fruit of her impregnable resolve. She had been hurt by Mellony's rebellion, but not influenced by so much as a hair's-breadth.

Early one morning, two or three days later, Mrs. Pember, lying awake waiting for the light to grow brighter that she might begin her day, heard a slight sound outside, of a certain incisiveness out of proportion to its volume. With an idleness that visited her only at early day-break, she wondered what it was. It was repeated, and this time, moved by an insistent curiosity blended with the recognition of its probable cause, she rose and looked out of the window which was close to the head of her bed. A little pier was a stone's throw from the house on that side, at which were moored several boats belonging to the fishermen about. It was as she thought; a stooping figure, dim and hazy in the morning fog, which blurred the nearest outlines and veiled the more distant, was untying one of the boats, and had slipped the oars into the rowlocks.

"Going fishing early," she said to herself. "I wonder which of 'em it is. They are all alike in this light."

Then she stood and looked out upon the morning world. It would soon be sunrise. Meanwhile, the earth was silent, save for the soft rippling of the untired waves that scarcely rose and fell in this sheltered harbor; the land had been at rest through the short night, but they had climbed and lapsed again steadily through its hours; the paling stars would soon have faded into the haze. The expectation of the creature waited for the manifestation.

Softly the boat floated away from its moorings. It seemed propelled without effort, so quietly it slipped through the water. In the bottom lay the sail and the nets, a shadowy mass; the boat itself was little more than a shadow, as it glided on into the thicker fog which received and enveloped it, as into an unknown vague future which concealed and yet held promise and welcome.

Mrs. Pember glanced at the clock. It was very early, but to go back to bed was hardly worth while. The sun was already beginning to glint through the fog. She dressed, and, passing softly the door of the room where Mellony slept,—rather fitfully of late,—began to make the fire.

The morning broadened and blazed into the day, and the whole town was making ready for its breakfast. Mellony was later than usual,—her mother did not hear her moving about, even; but she was unwilling to disturb her; she would wait a while longer before calling her. At last, however, the conviction of the immorality of late rising could no longer be ignored, and she turned the knob of Mellony's door and stepped into the room.

She had been mistaken in supposing that Mellony was asleep; the girl must have risen early and slipped out, for the room was empty, and Mrs. Pember paused, surprised that she had not heard her go. It must have been while she was getting kindling-wood in the yard that Mellony had left by the street door. And what could she have wanted so early in the village?—for to the village she must have gone; she was nowhere about the little place, whose flatness dropped, treeless, to the shore. Her mother went again to the kitchen, and glanced up and down the waterside. There was no one on the little wooden pier, and the boats swung gently by its side, their own among them, so Mellony had not gone out in that. Yes, she must have gone to the village, and Mrs. Pember opened the front door and scanned the wandering little street. It was almost empty; the early morning activity of the place was in other directions.

With the vague uneasiness that unaccustomed and unexplained absence always produces, but with no actual apprehension, Mrs. Pember went back to her work. Mellony had certain mild whims of her own, but it was surprising that she should have left her room in disorder, the bed unmade; that was not like her studious neatness. With a certain grimness Mrs. Pember ate her breakfast alone. Of course no harm had come to Mellony, but where was she? Unacknowledged, the shadow of Ira Baldwin fell across her wonder. Had Mellony cared so much for him that her disappointment had driven her to something wild and fatal? She did not ask the question, but her lips grew white and stiff at the faintest suggestion of it. Several times she went to the door, meaning to go out, and up the street to look for her daughter, but each time something withheld her. Instead, with that determination that distinguished her, she busied herself with trifling duties. It was quite nine o'clock when she saw Captain Phippeny coming up the street. She stood still and watched him approach. His gait was more rolling than ever, as he came slowly towards her, and he glanced furtively ahead at her house, and then dropped his eyes and pretended not to have seen her. She grew impatient to have him reach her, but she only pressed her lips together and stood the more rigidly still. At last he stood in front of her doorstone, his hat in his hand. The yellow shirt and the leathern jacket were more succinctly audacious than ever, but doubt and irresolution in every turn of his blue eyes and line of his weather-beaten face had taken the place of the tolerant kindliness.

"It's a warm mornin', Mis' Pember," he observed, more disconcerted than ever by her unsmiling alertness.

"You came a good ways to tell me that, Captain Phippeny."

"Yes, I did. Leastways I didn't," he responded. "I come to tell you about—about Mellony."

"What about Mellony, Captain Phippeny?" she demanded, pale, but uncompromising. "What have you got to tell me about Mellony Pember?" she reiterated as he paused.

"Not Mellony Pember," gasped the captain, a three-cornered smile trying to make headway against his embarrassment as he recalled the ancient tale of breaking the news to the Widow Smith; "Mellony Baldwin."

"Mellony Baldwin!" repeated Mrs. Pember, stonily, not yet fully comprehending.

The captain grew more and more nervous.

"Yes," he proceeded, with the haste of despair, "yes. Mis' Pember, you see Mellony—Mellony's married."

"Mellony married!" Strangely enough she had not thought of that. She grasped the doorpost for support.

"Yes, she up and married him," went on the captain more blithely. "I hardly thought it of Mellony," he added in not unpleasurable reflection, "nor yet of Ira."

"Nor I either." Mrs. Pember's lips moved with difficulty. Mellony married! The structure reared with tears and prayers, the structure of Mellony's happiness, seemed to crumble before her eyes.

"And I was to give you this;" and from the lining of his hat the captain drew forth a folded paper.

"Then you knew about it?" said Mrs. Pember, in a flash of cold wrath.

"No, no, I didn't. My daughter's boy brought this to me, and I was to tell you they was married. And why they set the job onto me the Lord he only knows!" and Captain Phippeny wiped his heated forehead with feeling; "but that's all I know."

Slowly, her fingers trembling, she unfolded the note.

"I have married Ira, mother," she read. "He took me away in a boat early this morning. It was the only way. I will come back when you want me. If I am to be unhappy, I'd rather be unhappy this way. I can't be unhappy your way any longer. I'm sorry to go against you, mother; but it's my life, after all, not yours,

Mellony."

As Mrs. Pember's hands fell to her side and the note slipped from her fingers, the daily tragedy of her married life seemed to pass before her eyes. She saw Captain Pember reel into the house, she shuddered at his blasphemy, she felt the sting of the first blow he had given her, she cowered as he roughly shook Mellony's little frame by her childish arm.

"She'd better be dead!" she murmured. "I wish she was dead."

Captain Phippeny pulled himself together. "No, she hadn't,—no, you don't, Mis' Pember," he declared stoutly. "You're making a mistake. You don't want to see Mellony dead any more'n I do. She's only got married, when all's said and done, and there's a sight of folks gets married and none the worse for it. Ira Baldwin ain't any great shakes,—I dono as he is; he's kinder light complected and soft spoken,—but he ain't a born fool, and that's a good deal, Mis' Pember." He paused impressively, but she did not speak. "And he ain't goin' to beat Mellony, either; he ain't that sort. I guess Mellony could tackle him, if it came to that, anyhow. I tell you, Mis' Pember, there's one thing you don't take no reckonin' on,—there's a difference in husbands, there's a ter'ble difference in 'em!" Mrs. Pember looked at him vaguely. Why did he go on talking? Mellony was married. "Mellony's got one kind, and you—well," he went on, with cautious delicacy, "somehow you got another. I tell you it's husbands as makes the difference to a woman when it comes to marryin'."

Mrs. Pember stooped, picked up the note, turned and walked into the living-room and sat down. She looked about her with that sense of unreality that visits us at times. There was the chair in which Mellony sat the night of her rebellious outbreak,—Mellony, her daughter, her married daughter. Other women talked about their "married daughters" easily enough, and she had pitied them; now she would have to talk so, too. She felt unutterably lonely. Her household, like her hope, was shattered. She looked up and saw that Captain Phippeny had followed her in and was standing before her, turning his hat in his brown, tattooed hands.

"Mis' Pember," he said, "I thought, mebbe, now Mellony was married, you'd be thinkin' of matrimony yourself agen." As Mrs. Pember gazed at him dumbly it seemed as if she must all at once have become another person. Matrimony had suddenly become domesticated, as it were. Her eyes travelled over the horseshoe charm and the long gold chain, as she listened, and from pocket

41

to pocket. "And so I wanted to say that I'd like to have you think of me, if you was making out the papers for another v'yage. The first mate I sailed with, she says to me when she died, 'You've been a good husband, Phippeny,' says she. I wouldn't say anythin' to you, I wouldn't take the resk, if she hadn't said that to me. Mis' Pember, and I'm tellin' it to you now because there's such a difference; and I feel kinder encouraged by it to ask you to try me. I'd like to have you marry me, Mis' Pember."

It was a long speech, and the captain was near to suffocation when it was finished, but he watched her with anxious keenness as he waited for her to reply. The stern lines of her mouth relaxed slowly. A brilliant red geranium in the window glowed in the sunlight which had just reached it. The world was not all dark. The room seemed less lonely with the captain in it, as she glanced around it a second time. She scanned his face: the buttonhole of a mouth had a kindly twist; he did not look in the least like handsome Dick Pember. Mellony had married, and her world was in fragments, and something must come after.

"I never heard as you weren't a good husband to Mis' Phippeny," she said calmly, "and I dono as anybody'll make any objection if I marry you, Captain Phippeny."

42

Memoir of Mary Twining

THE other day I spent several hours in looking over a lot of dusty volumes which had fallen to me in the way of inheritance. In the somewhat heterogeneous collection I came upon a brief memoir which, after a glance within, I laid aside as worthy, at least, of perusal. The other books were of little value of any sort—an orthodox commentary, an odd volume of a county history, one or two cook-books, a worn and broken set of certain standard British authors,—the usual assortment to be found in a country farmhouse, whose occupants soon ceased to keep up with the times. But this little book seemed to me unusual,—an opinion subsequently confirmed by examination. I had long ago discovered the fallacy of that tradition of early youth that a memoir is, of necessity, dull, and I was in nowise unfavorably affected by the title, "Memoir of Mary Twining." There proved to be something to me singularly quaint and charming in this little sketch, something fresh and new in this voice from bygone years. The subject of the memoir attracted me powerfully, both from the simplicity and naturalness of her own words, and the freedom and occasional depth of both thought and expression, in a day when freedom and thinking for one's self were less the fashion of New England maidens than they have since become. Or, it may be that the Editor, notwithstanding an occasional stiffness and apparent want of sympathy, has so well done his work, has understood so well what to give us and what to keep from us, that the reader's interest is skilfully fostered from the start. Be this as it may, I have not been able to resist the temptation to write, myself, a little of this memoir and its subject, to make a little wider, if I may, the public who have been told the story of this life. Not that it was an exciting or an eventful one, though lived in stirring times, but as I have already said, it seems to have a certain charm which should not be left forgotten in country garrets or unnoticed in second-hand bookstores. With no further apology for this review of it, I shall let the book, as far as possible, speak for itself.

Mary Twining was born in Middleport, Massachusetts, June 27, 1757. Her father fought with Colonel Washington in the French and Indian War, and subsequently under General Washington in a later disturbance. Her mother was a granddaughter of one of the early colonial governors. Mary seems to have come naturally enough by fine impulses and good breeding.

"It is not," says the conscientious biographer, "from any vain Partiality for high-sounding names, or any poor Pretense of good blood, which were most out of place in this our Republic, made so by the Genius and enduring Fortitude of all classes of Men, that I claim for Mary Twining stately Lineage, but that when such Accidents fall in the lives of Human Beings, it is not a thing to make light of, but worthy of study in its Results. Besides which is General Washington none the less a Good Soldier in that he is a Gentleman."

I suspect the traditions of a loyal Englishman had not been wholly eradicated from the mind of this biographer by a few years of plebeian institutions. With equal truth he goes on, however, to say that what was "of an Importance swallowing up the Lesser

Matter of Lineage and Station, Richard Twining was an upright and a God-fearing man, and Mary, his wife, patterned in all things after the Behaviour of her godly Ancestor." Either Richard or Mary, his wife, must have something "patterned" after a liberal and occasionally self-willed model, else whence came the spice of independence in the little Mary's character? She was an only child, and only children were probably in the middle of the eighteenth very much what they are in the close of the nineteenth century,—little beings allowed greater liberties, and burdened with heavier accountabilities, than where there are more to divide both. There are several incidents told of her childhood, not particularly remarkable, perhaps, but showing that her mind and her imagination were alive. She was not by any means a precocious child; her mind was but little, if at all, in advance of her years. If one may judge from detached anecdotes and descriptions, she showed no more than the receptivity and quickness natural to a bright and somewhat unusually clear intellect. Through all these anecdotes there runs a vein denoting what is less common in childhood than a certain precocity,—a keen sense of justice. She appears to have reasoned of many things, usually taken by childhood for granted, and assented to their results only if they seemed to her childishness just. If after life showed her that the affairs of this life can be but seldom regulated according to the ideas of finite justice, she never seems to have lost a certain fairness of judgment and opinion, which is rare in one of her sex and circumstances. When five years old, her mother, wishing her to give up a pet doll to a little crippled friend, told her that sympathy should suggest her doing it; that it was a privilege to make another happy; that it was selfishness to prefer her own pleasure of possession to that of another. But Mary listened unmoved to these arguments. Nevertheless the struggle was not a long one. With a good grace, after a few moments of silence, she carried the doll to her unfortunate friend. "Mamma," she said soberly, "she shall have it, for it is right that she should. I feel it. I shall have many things that she can never have."

For the logic of five years it was no small thing to have settled this question in this way. It would take too much time and too much space to dwell on the anecdotes of her childhood. Indeed, the biographer does not linger on them long himself.

"It is meet," he says, "to speak of these early Years, not from a desire to show that there was aught in the Childhood of Mary Twining remarkable or unnatural, that should be the Cause of Wonder or Admiration. But the rather that there may be evinced the Presence, even in the Germ, of certain Qualities of Soundness of Judgment and of Thoughtfulness unusual in a Female, which grew with her Growth, and which were in later Years, developed into stronger Traits by no unnatural means."

In 1773 she was sent away to a school in which she remained three years, varied by occasional visits at home. She made several friends here, and here, for the first time, kept a methodical and somewhat extended diary. From this diary her biographer makes copious extracts. In fact, from this period the memoir is chiefly made up from her several journals, in whose continuity there are now and then large gaps, with occasional notes. I shall make less copious extracts, principally those bearing upon that matter of which we always, more or less consciously, seek traces in the lives of individuals, distinguished or obscure, the love story. But first for her school life, into which few whispers of sentiment penetrated. It was no fashionable boarding-school to which she was sent, attended by young ladies whose dreams of what they will soon be doing in society monopolize the hours nominally devoted to literature and the sciences. An old friend of her mother opened her house to a few representatives of those families with whom she was acquainted, where, under the best teachers the country afforded, they were trained in such acquirements as wereprescribed by the canons of the day. On the fifteenth of September she says:—

"I have been something more than a week at the good School which my kind Parents have chosen for me. There seems, after all, to be little doing here. The few exercises in Mathematics, and the selections from the works of the most Highly Endowed of the Authors of England appear to me to be the most Profitable. As for the matter of Embroidery, I worked with Patience, ten years ago, a Sampler which was not considered discreditable, and it seems to me that of the multiplying of Stitches there is no end, and it were, perhaps, as well to go no farther. My daily Practice on the Spinet, may, perhaps, be the means of giving Pleasure at some Future Time, but it is the Occasion of but little Benefit in the Present, and of the Future can we be never certain."

The question of profitableness of a good many of her employments was often in her mind during these three years. She cannot help feeling that there are times when it is hard to contentedly fold the hands over even the worsted marvels of a "not discreditable" sampler. A year later, she says again:—

"More Practice and more Embroidery this afternoon. There are those of my Companions who ask nothing better than such unvarying Exercises. In them they find room for the employing of their Imagination and their Spirit. I wonder if it be so great a Fault in me, that I find them wearying. It is not that they are in themselves so distasteful, as it is that there seemeth much work waiting to be done, which a woman's Hands might well do, were it not reckoned somewhat unseemly."

"Her's was a somewhat restless Soul," says her biographer, "perplexing itself with Questions which it was not for her to answer."

Yes, with questions with which many a restless woman's soul has since perplexed itself, and which are now only beginning to attain solution. It is pleasant to find, in these early times, when we fancy New England maidens well content with their spinning and bread-making, hints that there were enterprising spirits who thought the prescribed round a too narrow one.

She finds some fault with one of her teachers for being too lenient with her.

"I received no Reproof," she says, "to-day when I most Richly deserved it. A Disturbance in the Hour for Study was entirely of my own making, but the Person who is Master at that Hour refused, with Persistence, to see it. I made it most evident, but he remarked, with a frown for a less Offender, that he should hold Mistress Twining excused. I shall find Occasion to address him on this Subject, for if I receive due Credit for that which I do that is

Well Done, I shall show no unwillingness to bear the Brunt of my Superior's Displeasure for what is Ill Done. Moreover, I will not have it otherwise."

"It were better," is the brief comment, "it were better had Mary Twining shown more Regret for what she herself confesses was ill done, rather than that she should take upon herself to correct the Faults of those towards whom she was somewhat lacking in Reverence." But it is droll enough to fancy the scene—the pretty schoolgirl gravely rebuking her delinquent master for the too great partiality her own bright eyes had won for her. Poor man! His was no sinecure. To hold rule over a parcel of unruly girls, with the graces of one so tugging at his heartstrings! His path might at least have been spared the thorn of having his fault denounced by the very voice that had done the mischief.

During the last year of her stay she writes less. Did the objectlessness of this education of hers pall upon the energy of her nature more and more? Or was her woman's heart preparing the way for the answer to this restless questioning? It is only now and then that we catch a glimpse of this development, which was singularly mature and singularly free from restriction.

"I have read many Tales," she says, "how true, in my small Experience, I know not, of the aptitude of Women, particularly those young women whose characters are in a state of most Imperfect Development, to yield in matters essential to their best Happiness to the Opposing Wishes of Parents and Guardians. I speak of those Matters, perhaps not the most fitting for the Speculations of a but Partially-schooled Maiden—Love, and the

Choosing of a Husband. While in these matters, as in all others, the Wishes of Wise and Fond Parents and Guardians are the only safe Guides for a young and Untrained Spirit, there are other Cases where Injustice and a Desire to Rule are but slender Grounds for the exercise of Authority. I know that my Boldness in this Opinion cannot pass even my own mind unchallenged, but when I read of Unwilling Maids forced to the very Church Door or Languishing under unmerited sternness, and Yielding up their own Happiness, and that of another (though he be a Man) into the Hands of an unwise Judge through inability to resist such unloving Pressure, my Nature rebels against it. It would seem to me cause for a Glad and an Unfaltering Resistance. For a Husband is, after all, a Matter for a Maid's own choosing."

"The beaten path," says the biographer, "had ever but little attraction for Mary Twining. It had been well had she been less fain to seek Opportunity for a Lawful Resistance to Bonds. It seemeth ever to the Young that such opportunities are not long in coming."

It was not only from the consciences of the colonial fathers that the stirrings of independence went forth. Apparently there was a spirit abroad that breathed now and then from the lips of but partially-schooled maidens. Still, it is not unruliness, this protest of a young and independent spirit against the slavishness now and then upheld in certain forms of literature. There is little revolutionary, after all, in Mary's sentiment that "a Husband is a matter for a Maid's own choosing."

But we must pass over the last few notes of her school life. At nineteen she left school forever.

"I am about to leave this little Life of School," she writes, "for a larger Life of Home, and mayhap a Taste of that Life which is called of the World. And if I be not now, at the age of Nineteen years, equipped for the change and able to comport myself with a becoming Discretion and Dignity, then such equipment is not to be found within these Four Walls or in daily Practice of Music and Mathematics. Which, though I be filled with no over-weening Distrust of my own Capabilities, seemeth to my eyes of some Doubt and Difference of Opinion."

"On a certain day of June," her biographer goes on to state, "Mistress Mary Twining was placed in the Coach which should take her a Two Days' Journey to her Father's House. She was in Company with an old and Reverend Gentleman of friendly Disposition, who was well known to her Father and held in excellent esteem of him. The Fairness of a Maid is but a vain Toy, but," declares this most staid biographer, with a refreshing candor, "as it is a matter which is not without its effect on the Fortunes of many, it is not always to be passed over in the Silence which would befit a Sober Pen. Mary Twining's Hair was of a golden Colour and wound itself in small, and not always tidy, Rings about her Neck and Forehead. Her eyes were of a darker appearance than is common, and her Mouth, though not without a certain Winsomeness, gave Promise of a Firmness of Opinion and an Independence which was perhaps but a Sign of the Times, which her small and shrewdly-set Nose did not deny."

I more than suspect that, disclaim it as he may, our discreet biographer was in nowise loath to dwell a little on this vain toy of Mary's personal appearance. I even fancy that he was tempted to employ greater latitude of expression, which only his stern sense of his responsibilities led him to reject, in the description of that uncompromising mouth, not to mention the spice of naughtiness involved in that nose so "shrewdly set."

Not an unattractive picture in the coach window, this June day, is this of Mary Twining, in her big poke bonnet, white kerchief and short-waisted gown. And who is this, who, coming at the last moment, springs into a vacant place at her side, under the very eyes of the reverend old gentleman, her father's friend? The three-cornered hat which he doffs with ceremonious courtesy to the fair vision before him, the powdered queue, the high boots with jingling spurs, the sword at his side, are not unpicturesque items in our nineteenth-century eyes. Were they likely to be so in the eyes of this nineteen-year-old maiden just out of boarding-school?

"As it happened," says the biographer, "there went down the same day, and by the same Coach, one of the young Aids of our General. He was a personable Youth, and the Arrangement of the many Fripperies of the Costume of a young Gallant did naught to take away from the Face and Figure which Providence had accorded him. It were better had he or Mary Twining chosen another Time for the Journey."

Neither, probably, did a natural timidity of disposition do aught to lessen the impression which a personable young man has it in his power in any century to make upon a fair and observing girl. Mary herself says:—

"There rode down with us a young gallant of most holiday Appearance, but not ignorant withal of the working days of a Soldier. It was not long before he had entered into Conversation with Mr. Edwards, who had knowledge of the young Man's Parents, from which Conversation I learned something of himself, though most modestly told. He would fain have opened the Way for me to join in my Guardian's Questioning, but I bore in Mind the Unseemliness of an unwarranted Acquaintanceship, and sought rather to avoid than to court the Glances which he was not over cautious in sending in my Direction."

"A Maid's avoidance," observes the biographer, "of a Youth's Glances, is not of that Nature that is the Cutting off of all Hope."

And Fortune, too, was not of so perverse a disposition in this June weather as she is sometimes. For, on the second day, when probably glances, so conscientiously evaded, had become but the accompaniment of spoken words, there was an accident. The coach, as coaches are apt to do, was upset, and its occupants "made haste rather as they could than as they would," to leave it. In the confusion and tumbling about of heavy boxes Mary might have been badly hurt, had not the young gallant, quickly springing to his feet, caught her as she was thrown forward by a second lurch of the unwieldy thing, and, lifting her up, carried her out of the way of falling luggage and struggling horses to a place of safety.

"He lifted me as though I had been but a Feather's weight, showing a Strength which is indeed Goodly in the Sons of Men," says Mary demurely, "and which was most grateful in the Stress and Confusion, and in its display most Timely, though perhaps," she adds, with delicious frankness, "he was not over ready to put me down that he might hasten back to be of further help."

"My Bonnet was awry," she continues, "my Hair in sad confusion, and my Face a Milkmaid Red, so that I said with but little Grace, 'Sir, I fear you have found me a grievous Weight.' Whereupon he answered me that so light was my weight, that his Heart was the Heavier for the Putting of me down, which was a Conceit not reasonable but most kindly intended. Whereon I thanked him, and he vowed such a Burden would he gladly carry to the World's End had he but Leave given."

Another picture not unpleasant to the mind's eye, the overturned coach, the esteemed guardian of the youthful beauty delaying a little in its immediate neighborhood, perhaps to secure the safety of some precious package, the farm laborers in the green adjacent fields dropping their tools and running forward to help, the outcry and confusion, and apart, in the summer sunshine, the handsome fellow with the flashing sword by his side, listening with bent head and admiring eyes to the thanks which Mistress Mary, with her untidy hair and lifted eyes, was tendering with "but little Grace."

"Such chance meeting of the Sexes," says our astute commentator, "where appear what is most commanding in the One and most dependent in the Other, are but ill advised. The Uttering of such vain proffers as the carrying the Burden of Mary Twining to the World's End, and other Foolishness, hath then a Savour of Reality which concealeth the vain Delusion."

We have delayed too long over these extracts, and though I am tempted to delay yet longer, so quaint is the contrast between Mary Twining's youthful and feminine pen and that of her critical biographer, I pass on to a time some months after her arrival home. Indeed, she writes little in the interval. The coming into a new and wider circle, the adapting herself to new conditions, leave her scant time for writing. There is a rapid noting of events, for it was an eventful time,—the mention of a few distinguished names, and that is all. But in order to follow the thread of Mary Twining's romance, we must pause at the account of a ball given to one of General Washington's regiments at a time before the rigor of war had quenched all thoughts of merry-making. It was not her first ball. She had mixed freely in society, and had measured herself with the men and women about her,—always an interesting experience to the free, unprejudiced and thoughtful girl.

"It was a joyous Scene enough," she writes, "but I myself not quite in the Humour for such Junketing. I had a gloomy Fancy that Reason would not dismiss, that in these Troublous Times there were Things outside of the Ball room Door, striving to enter, which having done, they would have proved of singular Inappositeness. None the less I danced with those who solicited me in due Form, and gave Heed to little else than the manner of the Solicitation. Not that there was Lack of Goodly Partners, but I was mindful of nothing beyond the Observance of the Courtesies of the Occasion.

The only Annoyance of which I was sensible was the marked Attention of my Cousin Eustace Fleming, who is but recently come into this our Part of the Country, and claimeth Relationship. He is a most excellent Young Gentleman, but one who is likely to weary me with his over Appreciation of my own Qualities. It is but a Sign of my Stubbornness and Unregeneracy of Heart that, in that he is most approved and commended of my Parents, he wearieth me the more. I was fain to tell him, when he asked me a third Time to join the Dance, that there were fairer Maidens in the Hall who would be less loth to accord him the Favour, but as this would but have drawn from him a laboured compliment to my own Person, I prudently refrained."

It was in the weariness of this very encounter that, looking up, she saw approaching her the hero of her adventure in the coach, the impulsive youth whose former foolishness had won for him the semi-disapproval of our commentator. It seems possible that the gloomy fancies of shadowy things outside lightened a little, and the war ceased to be a background only for shapes of evil.

"It required not the space of a moment for me to recognize him, though his Attire had changed with the Circumstance, but as my Father's Friend, Mr. Edwards, had not deemed it of sufficient Importance to mention our former Rencontre, it now seemed to me useless to publicly recall that Incident. Particularly as being now duly presented to me in the Presence of my Parents, and with due Vouchers of his Credit, our Acquaintance could make such Progress as we should mutually consider profitable."

Prudent Mistress Mary and delinquent Mr. Edwards!

"After the Cotillion for which he had asked the Honour of my Hand, he led me to my Seat, but by a somewhat indirect Route. Upon my remarking upon which, he found Occasion to say that all Ways were short to him now after traversing the long and difficult one which he had followed that he might gain Admission to my Presence. I, laughing, said that my Presence were hardly worth such effort in Gaining, and that it was generally attained with more Ease, and he, replying with a Grace of Manner it were impossible not to remark, said hastily that he was well aware that he had found it easier to enter than he should to again forsake it."

"And so on with such Vanities," says the biographer, "as pass Current with young Men and Maidens in their shortsighted Enjoyment of the moment, and with which Mary Twining was but too fain to dally."

Yes, and so on, the old story. For there follow the frequent meetings, known and not unapproved of by the watchful parents, the half confessions, the vague wonderment, and at last the pledge given and received, and Mary Twining became the affianced wife of the handsome young officer. All this we trace in her journal, with satiric comments, now and then, of the Editor; but it is all so familiar that we will not dwell on it, pretty as it is. Only one shadow seems to have fallen on the lovers,—that of Mr. Eustace Fleming, the worthy cousin, whose importunities in the ball-room so tired the patience of Mistress Mary. The parentally favored candidate for Mary's hand, he finds it, evidently, too hard to give it up without a struggle. With a lack of that wisdom unfortunate lovers find it so hard to supply, he disturbed their interviews, forced himself on Mary's society, yet with no insolence and no self-betrayal that could lead to an outbreak. He is apparently a self-contained, and not a bad man, who finds it impossible to see that he is beaten. Of this period I make one or two extracts from Mary's journal, and then go on to the end.

"If I once marvelled at the yielding of those weak Women who find it easier to relinquish the Happiness that they find in the Love of Those bound to them by mutual attraction, than to contest the matter with all Dignity, Forbearance, Firmness and Patience, how much the more do I marvel now at their Shortsightedness! Were he, whom I gladly call my Betrothed, to be the Victim of Oppression or of Malice, it would seem to me but the throwing down of the Glove—a challenge to Battle, rather than a demand for Submission. Methinks it were not as a Suppliant that I should stoop to pick it up. But why talk of fighting, who am a peaceful Maid, who would labour, were it but Honourable towards her dear Country, to remove the Sound of Battle far from her Lover. For indeed he is more ready to fight than am I to have him. He would see an Opportunity to strike a Blow in my Cause where is none, so anxious is he to draw his Sword in my Behalf. Indeed so excellent an Opinion doth he entertain of my Person and my Mind and my Conditions, that he would not be long in finding one who should most justly contest the same. Heaven send that he may hold to the Opinion and forget the Wish to make Proselytes!

"It would seem that some men were created but as a sort of Makeweight, who, without active Hindrance, make it more difficult to row one's Boat up the Stream of Life. Of such kind is my Cousin Eustace Fleming. His most mistaken Admiration of me (for that in him is a Mistake which in Another is but a most fitting and a most reverenced Creed) serves but to make a Let and Hindrance where my satisfaction is concerned. I would that he could more easily learn the Lesson I have been at such Pains to mark out for him."

"It were vain," is the comment on the last passage, "to expect a Recognition of sober worth in the Day of Love and Ambition. And Mistress Twining, after the manner of her kind, pays but little Heed to lasting Affection before the Time comes when it shall be of Use to Her."

The wedding day approaches. Mary Twining does not lose her independence, though, woman like, she seems to enjoy losing herself in the love lavished upon her. Here and there are passages which show that in the warmth of her romance she thinks and judges and acts for herself, as she did in her school days. Mary Twining will never merge her individuality in that of another, however dear to her.

The entries grow briefer and more infrequent, as the month fixed upon for the marriage draws near. It is to be in June,—two years from that June when she rode down by coach, in the care of her father's friend.

"The day is fixed for the twenty-seventh of June," is the last entry but two in her journal. "Two years ago, Fate gave my Life into his Hands. At least, in giving it to him a second Time, Fate and I are at one."

The next entry is a month later. It is simply the statement,—

"May 24th. I have done my Cousin Eustace wrong." Then on—

"July 27th. And I am but twenty-one!"

And June comes and goes, and there is no word on her bridal day, no breathings of her new happiness from her ready pen. Is the book closed? Yes, but her biographer has a word to say.

"On the twenty-seventh of June, Mary A. Twining became the wife of her Cousin Eustace Fleming. Their Betrothal was but a short one, but in the eyes of her judicious Parents, there was no unseemly Haste. It had long been a cherished wish of their Hearts, and Eustace Fleming was a young man of Promise and of rare Discretion."

There it ends. The record of Mary Twining is finished. With Mary Fleming he has nothing to do. But where is the girl of ripened understanding, of freedom of thought, of directness of purpose? We do not know, for our biographer does not tell us. Was there a tragedy, and were the details too heart-breaking for even the stoical Editor to maintain his critical attitude?

Where is the gallant cavalier with his picturesque devotion, and his vain toys of pretty speech and gesture and his fiery and over-weening love and admiration for Mistress Mary Twining? He seemed to me a brave and loyal sort of young fellow enough. I cannot tell. Put the quaint old book back on the shelf, and let her romance rest again. But notwithstanding her husband of such promise and rare discretion, I cannot help sighing, "Poor Mary Twining!"

Fate and she had a difference, after all. And she was but twenty-one!

A Postlude

IT was almost time for the train to leave the station, and the seats were filling rapidly. The Irishwoman, with four children so near of a size that they seemed to be distinguished only by the variety of eatable each one was consuming, had entered the car and deposited her large newspaper bundle just inside the door, and driven her flock all into the little end seat, where they were stowed uncomfortably, one on top of another, gazing stolidly about the car. The young girl from the country who had been spending Sunday in town, and who was, consequently, somewhat overdressed for Monday morning, was wandering elegantly up and down the aisle, losing each possible place for a prospective better one, which became impossible before she reached it. The woman with a bag too large for her to carry, rested it on the arm of an occupied seat while she gazed vaguely about, indifferent to the fact that a crowd of impatient travellers of more concrete intentions were being delayed by her indecision. Meanwhile, among these disturbers of travel the man with a large bag passed rapidly along, found a place, put the bag in the rack, seated himself, and took out his newspaper. There is something in a man's management of a large travelling-bag in a railway train that leads the most unwilling to grudgingly yield him a certain superiority of sex.

An exchange of good-bys, low-voiced but with a decided note of hilarity, took place at the door, and two women entered the car, one looking back and nodding a final smiling farewell before she gave her mind to the matter in hand. They were attractive women, of late middle age, perhaps, not yet to be called old. One was large, with fine curves, gray bands of hair under her autumnal bonnet, and a dignity of bearing which suited her ample figure and melodious, rather deep voice; the other was paler, more fragile, her light hair only streaked with gray, and her blue eyes still shaded with a half-wistful uncertainty of what might be before her, which the years had not been able to turn altogether into self-confidence.

"You go on, Lucy," said the former, in her full, decided tones, pausing at the first vacant seat, "and see if there's a place for us to sit together farther down. I'll hold this for one of us. You take up less room than I do, you know, and it's easier for you to slip about;" and she laughed a little. There was a suggestion of laughter in the eyes and around the mouth of each of them. It indicated a subdued exhilaration unusual in the setting forth of women of their years and dignity. Lucy hesitated a moment, and then moved on somewhat timidly; but she had taken only a step when the man near whom they stood rose, and, lifting his hat, said: "Allow me, madam, to give you this seat for yourself and your friend. I can easily find another."

"Thank you; you are very good," replied the larger of the two women, her kindly gray eyes meeting his with an expression that led him to pause and put their umbrellas in the rack and depart, wondering what it was about some women that made a man always glad to do anything for them,—and it didn't make any difference how old they were, either.

"How nice people are!" said the one who had already spoken as they settled themselves. "That man, now—there wasn't any need of his doing that."

"He seemed to really want to," rejoined Lucy. "People always like to do things for you, Mary Leonard, I believe," she added, looking at her companion with affectionate admiration.

"I like to hear you talk," returned Mary Leonard, laughing. "If there ever was anybody that just went through the world having people do things for 'em, it's you, Lucy Eastman, and you know it."

"Oh, but I know so few people," said the other, hastily. "I'm not ungrateful—I'm sure I've no call to be; but I know so few people, and they've known me all my life; it's not like strangers."

"That hasn't anything to do with it," affirmed Mary Leonard, stoutly; "if there were more, it would be the same way. But I will say," she went on, "that I never could see why a woman travelling alone should ever have any trouble—officials and everybody are so polite about telling you the same thing over. I don't know why it is, but I always seem to expect the next one I ask to tell me something different about a train; and then everybody you meet seems just as pleasant as can be."

"Yes," assented Lucy Eastman, "like that baggageman. Did you notice how polite the baggageman was?"

"Notice it! Why, of course I did. And our trunks were late, and it was my fault, and so I told him, and he just hurried to pull them around and check them, and I was so confused, you know, that I made him check the wrong ones twice."

"Well, they were just like ours," said Lucy Eastman, sympathetically.

"Well, they were, weren't they? But of course I ought to have known. And he never swore at all. I was dreadfully afraid he'd swear, Lucy."

"Oh, dear!" exclaimed Lucy Eastman, distressed, "what would you have done if he'd sworn?"

"I'm sure I don't know," asserted Mary Leonard, with conviction, "but fortunately he didn't."

"He got very warm," said Lucy, reminiscently. "I saw him wiping his brow as we came away."

"I don't blame him the least in the world. I think he was a wonderfully nice baggageman, for men of that class are so apt to swear when they get very warm,—at least, so I've heard. And did you hear—"

"Tickets, ma'am," observed the conductor.

"There, I didn't mean to keep you waiting a minute;" and Mary Leonard opened her pocketbook, "but I forgot all about the tickets. Oh, Lucy, I gave you the tickets, and I took the checks."

"Yes, to be sure," said Lucy, opening her pocketbook.

"I'll put them in the seat for you, ladies, like this," said the conductor, smiling, "and then you won't have any more trouble."

"Oh, yes, thank you," said Lucy Eastman.

"What a nice conductor!" observed Mary Leonard.

"Did I hear what, Mary?—you were telling me something."

"Oh, about the baggageman. I heard him say to his assistant, 'Don't you ever git mad with women, Bobby. It ain't no use. If it was always the same woman and the same trunk, perhaps you could learn her sometime; but it ain't, and you've got to take 'em just as they come, and get rid of 'em the best way you can—they don't bear instruction.'"

Mary Leonard and Lucy Eastman threw back their heads and laughed; it was genuine, low, fresh laughter, and a good thing to hear. After that there was silence for a few moments as the train sped on its way.

"I declare," said Mary Leonard, at last, "I don't know when I've been in the cars before."

"I was just thinking I haven't been in the cars since Sister Eliza died, and we all went to the funeral," said Lucy Eastman.

"Why, that's—let me see—eight years ago, isn't it?"

"Eight and a half."

"Well, I'm glad you'll have a pleasanter trip to look back on after this."

"So am I; and I am enjoying this—every minute of it. Only there's so much to see. Just look at the people looking out of the windows of that manufactory! Shouldn't you think they'd roast?"

"Yes, they must be hotter than a fritter such a day as this."

"How long is it since you've been to Englefield, Mary?" asked Lucy Eastman, after another pause.

"Why, that's what I meant to tell you. Do you know, after I saw you, and we decided to go there for our holiday, I began to think it over, and I haven't been there since we went together the last time."

"Why, Mary Leonard! I had an idea you'd been there time and again, though you said you hadn't seen the old place for a long time."

"Well, I was surprised myself when I realized it. But the next year my cousins all moved away, and I've thought of it over and over, but I haven't *been*. I dare say if we'd lived in the same town we'd have gone together before this, but we haven't, and there it is."

"That's thirty-five years ago, Mary," said Lucy Eastman, thoughtfully.

"Thirty-five years! I declare, it still makes me jump to hear about thirty-five years—just as if I hadn't known all about 'em!" and Mary Leonard laughed her comfortable laugh again. "You don't say it's thirty-five years, Lucy! I guess you're right, though."

There was a moment's pause, and the laugh died away into a little sigh.

"We didn't think then—we didn't really *think*—we'd ever be talking about what happened thirty-five years ago, did we, Lucy? We didn't think we'd have interest enough to care."

"No," said Lucy, soberly, "we didn't."

"And I care just as much as I ever did about things," went on the other, thoughtfully, "only there seem more doors for satisfaction to come in at nowadays. It isn't quite the same sort of satisfaction, perhaps, that it used to be, not so pressed down and running over, but there's more of it, after all, and it doesn't slip out so easily."

"No, the bottom of things doesn't fall out at once, as it used to, and leave nothing in our empty hands."

"That sounds almost sad. Don't you be melancholy, Lucy Eastman."

"I'm not, Mary—I'm not a bit. I'm only remembering that I used to be."

"We used to go to the well with a sieve instead of a pitcher; that's really the difference," said Mary Leonard. "We've learned not to be wasteful, that's all."

"What fun we used to have," said Lucy, her eyes shining, "visiting your cousins!"

"It *was* fun!" said the other. "Do you remember the husking party at the Kendals' barn?"

"Of course I do, and the red ears that that Chickering girl was always finding! I think she picked them out on purpose, so that Tom Endover would kiss her. It was just like those Chickerings!" There was a gentle venom in Lucy Eastman's tones that made Mary Leonard laugh till the tears came into her eyes.

"Minnie Chickering wasn't the only girl that Tom Endover kissed, if I remember right," she said, with covert intention.

"Well, he put the red ear into my hands himself, and I just husked it without thinking anything about it," retorted Lucy Eastman, with spirit.

"Of course you did, of course you did," asseverated Mary Leonard, whereupon the other laughed too, but with reservation.

"And do you remember old Miss Pinsett's, where we used to go to act charades?"

"Yes, indeed, in the old white house at the foot of the hill, with a cupola. She seemed so old; I wonder how old she was?"

"Perhaps we shouldn't think her so old to-day. People used to wear caps earlier then than they do now. I think when they were disappointed in love they put on caps! Miss Pinsett had been disappointed in love, so they said."

"They will have old maids disappointed in love," said Lucy, with some asperity. "They will have me—some people—and I never was."

"I know you weren't. But I don't think it's as usual as it was to say that about old maids. It's more the fashion now to be disappointed in marriage."

There had been several stops at the stations along the road. The day was wearing on. Suddenly Lucy Eastman turned to her companion.

"Mary," she said, "let's play we were girls again, and going to Englefield just as we used to go—thirty-five years ago. Let's pretend that we're going to do the same things and see the same people and have the same fun. We're off by ourselves, just you and I, and why shouldn't we? We're the same girls, after all," and she smiled apologetically.

"Of course we are. We'll do it," said Mary Leonard, decidedly; "let's pretend."

But, having made the agreement, it was not so easy to begin. The stream of reminiscence had been checked, and a chasm of thirty-five years is not instantly bridged, even in thought.

"I hope they won't meet us at the station," said Mary Leonard, after a while, in a matter-of-fact voice. "We know the way so well there is no need of it."

"I hope not. I feel just like walking up myself," answered Lucy. "We can send our trunks by the man that comes from the hotel, just as usual, and it'll be cool walking toward evening."

"I'm glad we put off coming till the fall. The country's beautiful, and there isn't so much dust in case we"—she hesitated a moment—"in case we go on a picnic."

"Yes," replied Lucy, readily; "to the old fort. I hope we'll have a picnic to the old fort. I guess all the girls will like to go. It's just the time to take that drive over the hill."

"If we go," said Mary Leonard, slowly and impressively, "you'll have to drive with Samuel Hatt."

"Oh, I went with him last time," broke in Lucy, apprehensively. "It's your turn."

"But you know I just won't," said Mary Leonard, her eyes sparkling, and the dimples that, like Miss Jessie Brown, she had not left off, appearing and disappearing. "And somebody has to go with him."

"Perhaps they won't ask him."

"Oh, but they will. They always do, on account of his horses. It wouldn't be a picnic without Samuel Hatt."

Just then the train drew up at a small station. Lucy Eastman started as she read the name of the place as it passed before her eyes.

"Mary," said she, "this is where Mr. Hatt always used to get on the train. There are the Hatt Mills, and he goes up and down every day,—don't you remember? And how we were—we are—always afraid we'll meet him on the train."

"Of course," said Mary Leonard, leaning forward and scanning the platform with its row of idlers and its few travellers. "Well, he isn't here now. We are going to escape him this time. But my heart was in my mouth! I don't want Samuel Hatt to be the first Englefield person we meet."

They looked up with careless curiosity at the people who entered the train. There was a little girl with a bunch of common garden flowers following close behind a tired-looking woman, who had been, obviously, "spending the day;" a florid old gentleman with gold spectacles, who revealed a bald head as he removed his hat and used it for a fan,—they had seen him hurrying to the platform just before the train moved out; a commercial traveller, and a schoolboy.

"No," said Mary Leonard, "he isn't here this time."

The florid old gentleman took a seat in front of them and continued to fan himself. The conductor came through the car.

"Warm spell we're having for October, Mr. Hatt," he said, as he punched the commutation-ticket that was offered him.

Mary Leonard and Lucy Eastman gazed spellbound at the back of Mr. Hatt's bald head. They were too amazed to look away from it at each other.

"It—it must be his father," gasped Lucy Eastman. "He looks—a little—like him."

"Then it's his father come back!" returned Mary in an impatient whisper. "His father died before we ever went to Englefield; and, don't you remember, he was always fanning himself?"

Their fascinated gaze left the shiny pink surface of Samuel Hatt's head, and their eyes met.

"I hope he won't see us," giggled Lucy.

"I hope not. Let's look the other way."

In a few minutes Mr. Hatt rose slowly and portentously, and, turning, made a solemn but wavering way down the car to greet a man who sat just across the aisle from Mary Leonard. Both the women avoided his eyes, blushing a little and with the fear of untimely mirth about their lips.

As he talked with their neighbor, however, they ventured to look at him, and as he turned to go back his slow, deliberate glance fell upon them, rested a moment, and, without a flicker of recognition, passed on, and he resumed his place.

There was almost a shadow in the eyes that met again, as the women turned towards one another.

"I—I know it's funny," said Lucy, a little tremulously, "but I don't quite like it that we look to him just as he does to us."

"We have hair on our heads," said Mary Leonard. "But," she added, less aggressively, "we needn't have worried about his speaking to us."

"Englefield," shouted the brakeman, and the train rumbled into a covered station. Mary Leonard started to her feet, and then paused and looked down at her companion. This Englefield! This the quiet little place where the man from the hotel consented to look after their trunks while their cousins drove them up in the wagon—this noisy station with two or three hotel stages and shouting drivers of public carriages!

"Lucy," said she, sitting down again in momentary despair, "we've gone back thirty-five years, but we forgot to take Englefield with us!"

It did not take long, however, to adapt themselves to the new conditions. They arranged to stay at the inn that was farthest from the centre of things, and the drive out restored some of the former look of the place. It was near sunset; the road looked pink before them as they left the city. The boys had set fire to little piles of early fallen leaves along the sides of the streets, and a faint, pungent smoke hung about and melted into the twilight, and the flame leaped forth vividly now and then from the dusky heaps. As they left the paved city for the old inn which modern travel and enterprise had left on the outskirts, the sky showed lavender through a mistiness that was hardly palpable enough for haze. The browns and reds of the patches of woods in the near distance seemed the paler, steadier reproduction of the flames behind them. Low on the horizon the clouds lay in purple waves, deepening and darkening into brown.

"Mary," said Lucy Eastman, in a low tone, laying her hand on her companion's arm, "it's just the way it looked when we came the first time of all; do you remember?"

"Remember? It's as if it were yesterday! Oh, Lucy, I don't know about a new heaven, but I'm glad, I'm glad it isn't a 'new earth' quite yet!" There was a mistiness in the eyes of the women that none of the changes they had marked had brought there. They were moved by the sudden sweet recognition that seemed sadder than any change.

The next morning they left the house early, that they might have long hours in which to hunt up old haunts and renew former associations. Again the familiar look of things departed as they wandered about the wider, gayer streets. The house in which Mary Leonard's cousins had lived had been long in other hands, and the occupants had cut down the finest of the old trees to make room for an addition, and a woman whose face seemed provokingly foreign to the scene came out with the air of a proprietor and entered her carriage as they passed.

At another place which they used to visit on summer afternoons, and which had been approached by a little lane, making it seem isolated and distant, the beautiful turf had been removed to prepare a bald and barren tennis court, and they reached it by an electric car. Even the little candy-shop had become a hardware store.

"Of course, when one thinks of the Gibraltars and Jackson balls, it does not seem such a revolution," said Mary Leonard; but she spoke forlornly, and did not care much for her own joke. It looked almost as if their holiday was to be turned into a day of mourning; there was depression in the air of the busy, bustling active streets, through which the gray-haired women wandered, handsome, alert, attentive, but haunted by the sense of familiarity that made things unfamiliar and the knowledge of every turn and direction that yet was not knowledge, but ignorance.

"Look here, Lucy Eastman," said Mary Leonard at last, stopping decisively in front of what used to be the Baptist Church, but which was now a business block and a drug-store where you could get peach phosphate, "we can't stand this any longer. Let's get into a carriage right away and go to the old fort; that can't have changed much; it used to be dismantled, and I don't believe they've had time, with all they've done here, to—to mantle it again."

They moved towards a cab-stand—of course it was an added grievance that there was a cab-stand—but the wisdom of the prudent is to understand his way.

"Mary," said Lucy Eastman, detaining her, "wait a minute. Do you think we might—it's a lovely day—and—there's a grocer right there—and dinner is late at the hotel"—She checked her incoherence and looked wistfully at Mary Leonard.

"Lucy, I think we might do anything, if you don't lose your mind first. What is it, for pity's sake, that you want to do?"

"Take our luncheon; we always used to, you know. And we can have a hot dinner at the hotel when we come back."

Without replying, Mary Leonard led the way to the grocer's, and they bought lavish supplies there and at the bakery opposite. Then they called the cab.

"Do you remember, Lucy, we used to have to think twice about calling a cab, when we used to travel together, on account of the expense," said Mary Leonard, as they waited for it to draw up at the curbstone.

"Yes," answered Lucy; "we don't have to now." And then they both sighed a little.

But their smiles returned as they drove into the enclosure of the old fort. There they lay in the peaceful sun—the gray stones, the few cannon-balls, sunk in the caressing grass, with here and there a rusty gun, like a once grim, sharp-tongued, cruel man who has fallen somehow into an amiable senility.

"I read an article in one of the magazines about our coast defences," said Lucy Eastman, breathlessly; "how they ought to be strengthened and repaired and all, and I was quite excited about it and wanted to give a little money towards it, but I wouldn't for anything now, enemy or no enemy."

"Nor I, either," said Mary Leonard, after she had dismissed the driver with orders to call for them later in the day. They walked on over the crisp dry grass, and seated themselves on a bit of the fallen masonry. The reaches of the placid river lay before them, and the hum of the alert cricket was in their ears. Now and then a bird flew surreptitiously from one bush to another, with the stealthy, swift motion of flight in autumn, so different from the heedless, fluttering, hither-and-yon vagaries of the spring and early summer. The time for frivolity is over; the flashes of wings have a purpose now; the possibility of cold is in the air, and what is to be done must be done quickly.

"We almost always used to come in summer," said Lucy Eastman, "but I think it's every bit as pretty in the fall."

"So do I," assented Mary Leonard, as she looked down into a hollow where the purple asters grew so thick that in the half-dusk of the shadow they looked like magnified snowflakes powdered thickly on the sward. "And it hasn't changed an atom," she went on, as her eyes roamed over the unevenness of this combination of man's and nature's handiwork. "It's just as quiet and disorderly and upset and peaceful as it was then."

"Yes, look up there;" and Lucy Eastman pointed to the higher ramparts, on the edge of which the long grass wavered in the wind with the glancing uncertainty of a conflagration. "The last time I was here I remember saying that that looked like a fire."

After they had eaten their luncheon, which brought with it echoes of the laughter which had accompanied the picnic supper eaten in that very corner years ago, they seated themselves in a sheltered spot to wait. It really seemed as if the old gray walls retained some of the spirit of those earlier days, so gentle, so mirth-inspiring was the sunshine that warmed them.

"I'm so glad we came," said Mary,—they had both said it before,—as the sunny peace penetrated their very souls.

Four o'clock brought the cab, and they drove down the long hills, looking back often for a final glimpse of the waving grass and the gray stones. As they turned a sharp corner and lost sight of the old fort, Mary Leonard glanced furtively at her companion. Her own eyes for the second time that day were not quite clear, and she was not sorry to detect an added wistfulness in Lucy Eastman's gaze.

"Lucy," said she, and her voice shook a little, "I'm tired."

"So am I," murmured Lucy.

"And I don't ever remember to have been tired after a picnic at the old fort before."

"No more do I," said Lucy; and it was a moment before their sadness, as usual, trembled into laughter.

"Lucy Eastman," said Mary Leonard, suddenly, "this is the street that old Miss Pinsett used to live on—lives on, I mean. What do you say? Shall we stop and see Miss Pinsett?" The dimples had come back again, and her eyes danced.

Lucy caught her breath.

"Oh, Mary, if only she—" her sentence was left unfinished.

"I'll find out," said Mary Leonard, and put her head out of the window. "Driver," she called out, "stop at Miss Pinsett's."

The driver nodded and drove on, and she sank back pleased with her own temerity.

The cab stopped in front of the same square white house, with the cupola, and the same great trees in the front yard. Mary Leonard and Lucy Eastman clasped each other's hands in silent delight as they walked up the box-bordered path.

"Tell Miss Pinsett that Lucy Eastman and—and Mary Greenleaf have come to see her," they said to the elderly respectable maid. Then they went into the dim shaded parlor and waited. There were the old piano and the Japanese vases, and the picture of Washington which they had always laughed at because he looked as if he were on stilts and could step right across the Delaware, and they could hear their hearts beat, for there was a rustle outside the door—old Miss Pinsett's gowns always rustled—and it opened.

"Why, *girls!*" exclaimed old Miss Pinsett as she glided into the room.

Mary Leonard and Lucy Eastman declared, then and afterward, that she wasn't a day older than when they said good-by to her thirty-five years ago. She wore the same gray curls and the same kind of cap. Also, they both declared that this was the climax, and that they should have wept aloud if it had not been so evident that to Miss Pinsett there was nothing in the meeting but happiness and good fortune, so they did not.

"Why, girls," said old Miss Pinsett again, clasping both their hands, "how glad I am to see you, and how well you are both looking!"

Then she insisted on their laying off their things, and they laid them off because they always had when she asked them.

"You've grown stout, Mary Greenleaf," said old Miss Pinsett.

"I know I have," she answered, "and I'm not Mary Greenleaf, though I sent that name up to you—I'm Mary Leonard."

"I wondered if neither of you were married."

"I'm a widow, Miss Pinsett," said Mary Leonard, soberly. "My husband only lived three years."

"Poor girl, poor girl!" said Miss Pinsett, patting her hand, and then she looked at the other.

"I'm Lucy Eastman still," she said; "just the same Lucy Eastman."

"And a very good thing to be, too," said Miss Pinsett, nodding her delicate old head kindly. "But," and she scanned her face, "but, now that I look at you, not quite the same Lucy Eastman—not quite the same."

"Older and plainer," she sighed.

"Of all the nonsense!" exclaimed old Miss Pinsett. "You're not quite so shy, that's all, my dear."

"I'm shy now," asserted Lucy.

"Very likely, but not quite so shy as you were, for all that. Don't tell me! I've a quick eye for changes, and so I can see changes in you two when it may be another wouldn't."

Before the excitement of her welcome had been subdued into mere gladness, there was a discreet tap at the door, and the respectable maid came in with a tray of sherry-glasses and cake. Mary Leonard and Lucy Eastman looked at each other brimming over with smiles. It was the same kind of cake, and might have been cut off the same loaf.

"Never any cake like yours," said Mary Leonard.

"I remember you like my cake," said old Miss Pinsett, smiling; "take a bigger piece, child."

They wanted to know many things about the people and the town, all of which Miss Pinsett could tell them.

The shadows grew longer, the room dimmer, and Miss Pinsett had the maid throw open the blinds to let in the western sunlight. A shaft of illumination fell across one of the Japanese vases, and a dragon blinked, and the smooth round head of a mandarin gleamed. There was an old-fashioned trumpet-creeper outside the window.

"But we must go," exclaimed Mary Leonard at last, rising and taking up her bonnet. "Oh, no, thank you, we must not stay. Miss Pinsett; we are going to-morrow, and we are tired with all the pleasure of to-day, and we have so much—so much to talk over. We shall talk all night, as we used to, I am afraid."

"But before you go, girls," said Miss Pinsett, laying a fragile, white slender hand on each, "you must sing for me some of the songs you used to sing—you know some very pretty duets."

Mary Leonard and Lucy Eastman paused, amazed, and looked into each other's faces in dismay. Sing?—had they ever sung duets? They had not sung a note for years, except in church.

"But I don't know any songs, Miss Pinsett," stammered Mary Leonard.

"I have forgotten all I ever knew," echoed Lucy Eastman.

"No excuses, now—no excuses! You were always great for excuses, but you would always sing for me. I want 'County Guy,' to begin with."

By a common impulse the visitors moved slowly towards the piano; they would try, at least, since Miss Pinsett wanted them to. Lucy seated herself and struck a few uncertain chords. Possibly the once familiar room, Mary Leonard at her side, Miss Pinsett listening in her own high-backed chair, the scent of the mignonette in the blue bowl—possibly one or all of these things brought back the old tune.

"Ah, County Guy,
The hour is nigh,
The sun has left the lea."

The sweet, slender voice floated through the room, and Mary Leonard's deeper contralto joined and strengthened it.

"Now, I will have 'Flow Gently, Sweet Afton,'" said Miss Pinsett, quite as if it were a matter of course. And they sang "Flow Gently, Sweet Afton." It was during the last verse that the parlor door opened softly, and a tall, fine-looking man, erect, with beautiful silver curling hair, and firm lines about the handsome, clean-shaven mouth, appeared on the threshold and stood waiting. As the singing finished, Miss Pinsett shook her head at him.

"You were always coming in and breaking up the singing, Tom Endover," she said.

The two women left the piano and came forward.

"You used to know Mary Greenleaf,—she's Mrs. Leonard now,—and Lucy Eastman, Tom," she went on.

Apparently Mr. Endover was not heeding the introduction, but was coming towards them with instant recognition and outstretched hand. They often discussed afterward if he would have known them without Miss Pinsett. Mary Leonard thought he would, but Lucy Eastman did not always agree with her.

"You don't have to tell me who they are," he said, grasping their hands cordially. "Telling Tom Endover who Mary Greenleaf and Lucy Eastman are, indeed!" There was a mingling of courteous deference and frank, not to be repressed, good comradeship in his manner which was delightful. Mary Leonard's dimples came and went, and delicate waves of color flowed and ebbed in Lucy Eastman's soft cheeks.

"I'm too old always to remember that there's no telling a United States senator anything," retorted Miss Pinsett, with a keen glance from her dimmed but penetrating eyes.

"As to that, I don't believe I'd ever have been a United States senator if it wasn't for what you've told me, Miss Pinsett," laughed Endover. "I'm always coming here to be taken down, Mary," he went on; "she does it just as she used to."

Mary Leonard caught her breath a little at the sound of her Christian name, but "I didn't know there was any taking you down, Tom Endover," she retorted before she thought; and they all laughed.

They found many things to say in the few minutes longer that they stayed, before Mr. Endover took them out and put them in their cab. He insisted upon coming the next morning to take them to the station in his own carriage, and regretted very much that his wife was out of town, so that she could not have the pleasure of meeting his old friends.

"He's just the same, isn't he?" exclaimed Mary Leonard, delightedly, as they drove away.

"Yes," assented Lucy Eastman, slowly; "I think he is; and yet he's different."

"Oh, yes, he's different," replied Mary Leonard, readily. Both were quite unconscious of any discrepancy in their statements as they silently thought over the impression he had made. He was the same handsome, confident Tom Endover, but there was something gone,—and was there not something in its place? Had that gay courtesy, that debonair good fellowship, changed into something more finished, but harder and more conscious? Was there a suggestion that his old careless charm had become a calculated and a clearly appreciated facility? Lucy Eastman did not formulate the question, and it did not even vaguely present itself to Mary Leonard, so it troubled the pleasure of neither.

"What a day we have had!" they sighed in concert as they drove up again to the entrance of the inn.

"Lucy," called Mary Leonard, a little later, from one of their connecting rooms to the other, "I'm going to put on my best black net, because Tom Endover may call to-night." Then she paused to catch Lucy Eastman's prompt reply.

"And I shall put on my lavender lawn, but it'll be just our luck to have it Samuel Hatt."

The next morning Mr. Endover called for them, and they were driven to the station in his brougham.

He put them on the train, and bought the magazines for them, and waved his hand to the car window.

"You know, Lucy," said Mary Leonard, as the train pulled out, "Tom Endover always used to come to see us off."

"Of course he did," said Lucy.

"Do you know, I'm rather glad his wife was out of town," went on Mary Leonard, after a pause. "I should like to have seen her well enough, but you know she wasn't an Englefield girl."

"What can she know about old Englefield!" said Lucy, with mild contempt. "I'm very glad she was out of town."

As they left the city behind them, the early morning sun shone forth with vivid brilliancy. Against the western sky the buildings stood out with a peculiar distinctness, as if the yellow light shining upon them was an illumination inherent in themselves, singling them out of the landscape, and leaving untouched the cold gray behind them. The lines of brick and stone had the clearness and precision of a photograph, and yet were idealized, so that in the yellow, mellow, transparent light a tall, smoke-begrimed chimney of a distant furnace looked airy and delicate as an Italian tower.

The "Daily Morning Chronicle"

THE village lay still and silent under the observant sun. The village street stretched in one direction down the hill to the two-miles-off railway station, and in the other to the large white house with pillared portico, from which there was a fine view of the sunset, and beyond which it still continued, purposeful but lonely, until it came suddenly upon half a dozen houses which turned out to be another village.

Not a man, woman, or child crossed from one house to another; not a dog or a cat wandered about in the sunshine. The white houses looked as if no one lived in them; the white church, with its sloping approach, looked as if no one ever preached in it and no one ever came to it to listen. It seemed to Lucyet Stevens, as she sat at the little window of the post-office, behind which her official face looked so much more important than it ever did anywhere else, as if the village street itself were listening for the arrival of the noon mail. For it was nearly time for the daily period of almost feverish activity. By and by from the station would come Truman Hanks with the leather bag which, in village and city alike, is the outward and visible sign of the fidelity of the government. It is probable that he will bring it up in a single carriage, for though sometimes he takes the two-seated one, in case there should be a human arrival who would like to be driven up, this possibility was so slight a one at this time of year that it was hardly worth considering. Then the village will awake; the two little girls who live down below the saw-mill will come up together, confiding on the way a secret or two, for which the past twenty-four hours would seem to have afforded slender material. Then old John Thomas will come limping across from his small house back of the church, to see if there is a letter for "her,"—she being his wife, and in occasional communication with their daughter in the city. Then the good-looking, roughly clad young farmer who takes care of the fine place with the pillared portico on the hill will saunter down to see if "the folks have sent any word about coming up for the summer." Then Miss Granger, who lives almost next door, will throw a shawl over her head and run in to see who has letters and, incidentally, if she has any herself; and then one or two wagons will draw up in front of the little store, and the men will come in for their daily papers.

As Lucyet came around to the daily papers she flushed and looked impatiently out of the door down the street. Not that the thought of the daily paper had not been all the time in the background of her mind, but having allowed her fancy to wander towards the attitude of the village and its prospective disturbance, she returned to the imminence of the daily paper again with a thrill of emotion. It was not one of the metropolitan journals which, as a body, the village subscribed for, nor was it one of the more widely known of those issued in smaller cities; it was an unpretentious sheet, neither very ably edited nor extensively circulated,—the chief spokesman of the nearest county town. But with all its limitations, its readers represented to Lucyet the great harsh, unknowing, and yet irresistibly attractive public.

It was not the first time that she had thus watched for it with mute excitement. Such episodes, though infrequent, had marked her otherwise uneventful existence at irregular intervals for more than a year. It would be more correct to say that they had altered its entire course; that such episodes had given to her life a double character,—one side of calmness, secrecy, indifference, and the other of delight, absorption, thrilled with a breathless excitement and uncertainty. But this time there was a greater than ordinary interest. The verses that she had sent last were more ambitious in conception; they had description in them, and mental analysis, and several other things which very likely she would not have called by their right names, though she felt their presence: her other contributions had belonged rather to the poetry of comment. She was sure, almost sure, that they had accepted these.

Unsophisticated Lucyet never dreamed of enclosing postage for return, so she could only breathlessly search the printed page to discover whether her lines were there or in the waste-basket. Friday's edition of the "Daily Morning Chronicle" was more or less given over to the feeble claims of general literature. To-day was Friday. Lucyet glanced through her little window—the tastefully disposed corner of which was dedicated to the postal service—at the tin of animal crackers, the jar of prunes, the suspended bacon, and the box of Spanish licorice, and pondered, half contemptuously, half pitifully, on what had been her life before she had written poems and sent them to the "Daily Morning Chronicle." Then her outlook had seemed scarcely wider than that of the animal crackers with their counterfeit vitality; now it seemed extended to the horizon of all humanity.

There was the sound of horses' feet coming over the hill. Was it the mail wagon? No, it was a heavier vehicle; and the voice of the farmer, slow and lumbering as the animals it encouraged, sounded down the village street. Over the crest of the hill appeared the summit of a load of hay going to the scales in front of the tavern to be weighed. So silent were the place and the hour, that it was like a commotion when the cart drew up, and the horses were unhitched and weighed, and then the load driven on, and the owner and the hotel-keeper exchanged observations of a genial nature. Finally the horses and the wagon creaked along the hot street down the road which led by the pillared white house, and again the village was at peace. Lucyet glanced at the clock. Was the mail going to be late this morning? No. The creaking of the hay wagon had but just lost itself in the silence, when her quick ear caught the rattle of the lighter carriage. Her first impulse was to step to the door and wait for it there, but she did not yield to it; she would do just as usual, neither more nor less. She would not for worlds have Truman Hanks suspect any special interest on her part. He might try to find out its cause; and a hot blush enveloped Lucyet as she contemplated the possibility of his assigning it to the true one. Only one person in all the village knew that Lucyet Stevens wrote poetry.

"Most time for the mail to be gittin' heavy," said Truman, as he handed over the limp receptacle; "the summer boarders 'll be along now, before long."

"Yes, I s'pose they will," answered Lucyet, her fingers trembling as they unlocked the bag.

"It's a backward season, though," he went on, watching her.

"Yes, it is uncommon backward; the apple blossoms aren't but just beginning to come out."

It seemed to her that there was suspicion in his observation. He leaned lazily over the counter, while she took out the mail within the little office with its front of letter-boxes.

"This hot spell 'll bring 'em out. It's the first *hot* spell we've had."

"Yes," she assented, blushing again, "it will."

She had spoken of the tardy apple blossoms in her poem,—it was entitled "Spring." Two or three people, having seen the mail go by, dropped in and disposed themselves in various attitudes to wait for it to be distributed. She hurried through the work, her fingers tingling to open each copy of the newspaper as she laid it in its place. At last it was done; the little window which had been shut to produce official seclusion was reopened; and the people came up, one by one, without much haste, and received the papers and now and then a letter. It did not take long; and afterward they stood about and talked and traded a little, their papers unopened in their hands. It was not likely that the news from outside was going to affect any one of them very much; they could wait for it; and reading matter was for careful attention at home, not for skimming over in public places.

Lucyet found their indifference phenomenal; they did not know what might be waiting for them in the first column of the third page. Was it waiting for them? The suspense was almost overwhelming; and yet she did not like to open the copy which lay at her disposal until the store was empty; she had a nervous feeling that they would all know what she was looking for. Slowly the group melted away, till there was no one left except the proprietor, who had gone into the back room to look after some seed corn, and Silas, the young farmer, who had thrown himself down into a chair to read his paper at his leisure, and was not noticing Lucyet. Eagerly she opened the printed sheet. She caught her breath in the joy of assurance. There it was—"Spring." It stood out as if it were printed all in capitals. After a furtive look out at the quiet street, where, in a rusty wagon, an old man was just picking up his reins and preparing to jog away from the post-office door, and a side glance at Silas's broad back over by the farther window, Lucyet read over her own lines. How different they looked from the copy in her own distinct, formal little handwriting! They had gained something,—but they had lost something too. They seemed unabashed, almost declamatory, in their sentiment. They had acquired a new and positive importance; it was as if the assertions they made had all at once become truths, had ceased to be tentative. She read them over again. No, they did not tell it all, all that she meant to say; but they brought back the day, and she was glad she had written them,—glad with an agitated, inexpressible gladness. She would like to know what people said of them; for a moment it seemed to her that she would not mind if they knew that she wrote them.

"Well," said Silas, laying down his paper and standing up, "there isn't a blamed thing in that paper!"

Lucyet looked up at him startled. Had she heard aright? Then the color slowly receded from her face and left it pale. Silas was quite unconscious of having made an unusual statement.

"Well, Lucyet," he went on, "going to the Christian Endeavor to-night?"

"I don't know," she stammered. "No," she added suddenly, "I am not." All endeavor was a mockery to her stunned soul.

"I dunno as I will either," he observed carelessly as he lounged out.

It was nothing to her whether he went or not, though once it might have been. She sat still for some minutes after he had gone, looking blankly at the paper. The page which a few minutes ago had seemed fairly to glow with interest had become mere columns of print concerning trivial things; for an instant she saw it with Silas's eyes. John Thomas came limping for his mail. He had been detained on the way, he explained, and was late. She handed him his paper through the window, dully, indifferently. She was suffering a measure of that disappointment which comes with what we have grown to believe attainment, and is so much more bitter than that of failure. But the revolt against this unnatural state of mind came before long. The elasticity of her own enthusiasm reasserted itself. It could not be that there was nothing in her poem. She read the lines over again. Two or three were not quite what they ought to be, somehow; but the rest of them the world would lay hold of,—that big sympathetic world which knew so much more than Silas Stevens.

When the hour came to close the office at noon, she locked the drawer and passed out of the door to the footpath with a sense of triumph under the habitual shyness of her manner. She still shrank from the publicity she had achieved, but she was conscious of an undercurrent of desire that her achievement, since it was real, should be recognized.

When the old postmaster died, leaving Lucyet, his only child, alone in the world, and interest in official quarters had procured for her the appointment in her father's place, a home had also been offered her at Miss Flood's; and it was thither that Lucyet now went for her noonday meal. Miss Delia Flood was of most kindly disposition and literary tastes. That these tastes were somewhat prescribed in their manifestation was no witness against their genuineness. It must be confessed that Miss Delia's preference was for the sentimental,—though she would have modestly shrunk from hearing it thus baldly stated,—and, naturally, for poetry above prose. The modern respect for "strength" in literature would have impressed her most painfully had she known of it. The mind turns aside from the contemplation of the effect that a story or two of Kipling's would have produced upon her could she have grasped their vocabulary; she would probably have taken to her bed in sheer fright, as she did in a thunderstorm. Poetry of the heart and emotions, which never verged, even most distantly, upon what her traditions and her susceptibilities told her was the indecorous, satisfied her highest demands, and the less said about nature, except by way of an occasional willow, or the sad, sweet scent of a jasmine flower, the better. Miss Delia had fostered Lucyet's love for literature; and it was to Miss Delia that Lucyet hastened with the great news of the publication of her poem. It was for this acute pleasure that she had hitherto kept the knowledge of her attempt from her,—and, too, that her joy might be full, and that she would not have to suffer the alternating phases of hope and fear through which Lucyet herself had passed.

As she entered the room where dinner stood on the table and Miss Delia waited to eat it with her, she suppressed the trembling excitement which threatened to make itself visible in her manner now that the words were upon her very lips. They seated themselves at the table. Miss Delia was small and wiry and grave, and never spilled anything on the tablecloth when helping

"Miss Delia," said Lucyet, "I've written a poem."

Her companion looked at her and smiled a shrewd little smile. "I've guessed as much before now," she said.

"But," said Lucyet, laying down her knife and fork, "it has been printed."

"Printed, child!" exclaimed Miss Delia, almost dropping hers. At last the cup of satisfaction was at Lucyet's lips; at least she had not overestimated the purport of the event to one human being.

"Printed," repeated Lucyet, smiling softly. "Here it is in the paper."

Miss Delia pushed aside her plate, seized the paper, and, opening it, searched its columns. She had not to look long; there was but one poem. Lucyet watched with shining eyes. This is what it meant; this was the realization of her dreams—to see the reader pass over the rest of the page as trivial, to be arrested with spellbound interest at the word "Spring," to know that the words that held that absorbed attention were her words—her own.

As Miss Delia read, gradually her expression changed; from eagerness it faded into perplexity. Lucyet watched her breathlessly, her hands clasped, her thin arms and somewhat angular elbows resting on the coarse tablecloth. From perplexity Miss Delia's look was chilled into what the observant girl recognized, with a dull pain at her heart, as disappointment. Lucyet averted her gaze to a dish of ill-shaped boiled potatoes; there was no need of watching longer the face opposite. Miss Delia read it all through again, dwelling on certain lines, which she indicated by her forefinger, with special attention; then she looked up timidly. She met Lucyet's unsmiling eyes for a moment; then she, too, looked away, hurriedly, helplessly, to the dish of boiled potatoes.

"I'm sure it is very nice—very nice indeed, Lucyet," she said.

"But you don't like it," said Lucyet.

"Oh, yes, I do," poor Miss Delia hastened to say. "I do like it; the rhymes are in the right places, and all, and it looks so nice in the column." Mechanically she pulled her plate back again, and Lucyet did the same. "I'm proud of you, Lucyet," she went on with a forced little smile, "that you can write real poetry like that."

"But what if it isn't real poetry?" said Lucyet.

The doubt was wrung from her by the overwhelming bitterness of her disappointment. A rush of tears was smarting behind her rather inexpressive eyes; but she held them back. Miss Delia was thoroughly distressed. She put aside her own serious misgivings.

"But it must be," she argued eagerly, "or they wouldn't have printed it."

Lucyet shook her head as she forced herself to eat a morsel of bread. How unconvincing sounded the argument from another's lips! and yet she knew now that secretly it had carried with it more weight than she had realized. Miss Delia glanced apprehensively at the folded paper as it lay on the table. She herself was disappointed, deeply disappointed; she had expected much, and this,—why, this was, most of it, just what any one could find out for herself. But she must say something more. Lucyet's patient silence as she went on with her dinner, never raising the eyes which had so shone when she first spoke, demanded speech from her more urgently than louder claims.

"I suppose I thought perhaps there would be more about—about misfortune, and scattered leaves, and dells,"—poor Miss Delia smiled deprecatingly, while she felt wildly about for more tangible reminiscences of her favorite poets, that she might respond to the unuttered questioning of Lucyet,—"and"—she dropped her eyes—"lovers."

"I don't know anything about dells and lovers," said Lucyet, simply; "how should I?"

Miss Delia started a little. It had never occurred to her that one must know about things personally in order to write poetry about them. If it had, she would never have dreamed of mentioning lovers.

"No, of course not," she said hastily; "but writing about a thing isn't like knowing about it."

Lucyet was not experienced enough to detect any fallacy in this, and she dumbly acquiesced.

"You have in all the grass and trees and—and such things as you have in—very nicely, I'm sure," went on Miss Delia; "only next time"—and she smiled brightly—"next time you must put in what we don't see every day—like islands and reefs and such things. I know you could write a beautiful poem about a reef—a coral reef."

Lucyet tried to smile hopefully in return, but the attempt was a failure. She had finished her dinner, and she longed to get away; she was so hurt that she must be alone to see how it was to be borne. She helped Miss Delia clear the table and wash the dishes, almost in silence. Two or three times they exchanged words on indifferent subjects; Miss Delia asked who had had letters, and Lucyet told her, but it was hard work for both. When it was over, Lucyet paused in the doorway, putting on her straw hat to go back to the post-office.

Miss Delia stood a moment irresolute, and then stepped to her side. "Lucyet," she said, her voice trembling, "I don't understand it exactly. It isn't like the poetry I've been used to. There are things in it that I don't know what they mean. To be sure, that's so with all poetry that we do like,"—the tears were in her eyes; it is not an easy thing to disappoint one's best friend and to be conscious of it,—"but it isn't like what I thought it was going to be, just about what we see out of the window. But it's my fault, just as likely as not,"—she laid her hand on Lucyet's arm,—"that's what I want to say; you mustn't take it to heart—just 's likely 's not, it's my fault."

Miss Delia did not believe a word of what she was saying, which made it difficult for her to articulate; but she was making a brave effort in her sensitive loyalty.

"I know," said Lucyet, gently; "but I guess it isn't your fault;" and she slipped out to the road on her way to the post-office. Miss Delia went back, picked up the paper, and, seating herself at the window, she read "Spring" all through again, word by word; then she laid it aside again, shaking her head sadly.

Lucyet went quietly behind her little window. Her disappointment amounted to actual physical pain. She found no comfort, as a wiser person might have done, in certain of Miss Delia's expressions; she only realized that her best friend and her most generous critic could find nothing good in what she had done. Her duty this afternoon was only to make up the mail for the down train; then her time was her own till the next mail train came up at half-past five. At two o'clock she closed the office again and started on a long walk. She longed for the comfort of the solitary hillsides, where warm patches of sunlight lay at the foot of ragged stone walls, and there were long stretches of plain and meadow to be looked over, and rolling hills to comfort the soul. As she climbed a hill just before the place where a weedy untravelled road turned off from the highway leading between closely growing underbrush and stone walls, where now and then a shy bird rustled suddenly and invisibly among last year's dried leaves, she saw three countrymen standing by the wayside and talking with as near an approach to earnestness as ever visits the colloquies of the ordinary unemotional New Englander. One of them held a copy of the "Daily Chronicle," gesturing with it somewhat jerkily as he spoke.

For a moment the hope that it is hard to make away with revived in Lucyet's breast. Were they talking of the poem, she wondered, with a certain weary interest. She dreaded a fresh disappointment so keenly that it pained her to speculate much on the chance of it. It was not impossible that they were saying such meaningless stuff ought never to have been printed. As the pale girl drew near with the plodding, patient step which so often proclaims that walking is not a pleasure, but a necessity, of country life, the men did not lower their voices, which she heard distinctly as she passed.

"Wal, I tell you, 't was that," said one of them. "He didn't live more'n a little time after he took it."

"Mebbe he wouldn't have lived anyhow."

"Wal, mebbe he wouldn't. 'T ain't for me to say," responded the first speaker evincing a certain piety, which, however, was not to be construed as at variance with his first statement.

"Wal, 't wa'n't this he took, was it?" demanded the man with the "Chronicle," waving it wildly.

"Wal, no, 't wa'n't," responded the other, reasonably. The third member of the party maintained an air of not being in a position to judge, and regarded Lucyet stolidly as she approached.

"Do, Lucyet?" he observed, unnoticed of the other two.

"I tell you this'll cure him. It'll cure anybody. Just read them testimonies,"—and he pressed the paper into the other's meagre hand. "Read that one, 'Rheumatiz of thirty years' standin',—it'll interest ye."

Lucyet went on up the hill, and turned into the weedy road. She had not a keen sense of the ridiculous. It did not strike her as funny that they should have been discussing a patent medicine instead of the verses on "Spring;" but her shrinking sense of defeat was deepened, and she felt, with an unconscious resentment, that most people cared very little about poetry. She wondered, without bitterness, and with a saddened distrust of her own power, if she could write an advertisement. Once within the precincts of the tangled road, her disquieted soul rejoiced in the freedom from observation. She felt as bruised and sore from the unsympathetic contact of her world as if it had been a larger one; and with the depression had come a startled sense of the irrevocableness of what she had done. Those printed words seemed so swift, so tangible. They would go so far, and afford such opportunity for the grasp of indifference, of ridicule! If she could only have them again, spoken, perhaps, but unheard!

Yet here, at least, where the enterprising grass grew in the rugged cart track, and the branches drooped impertinently before the face of the wayfarer, no one but herself need know that she was very near to tears. And as she came out of the shut-in portion of the road to a stretch of open country, where the warm light lay on the hillsides, and the air was sweetened by the breath of pines, her depression gave way to a keen sense of elation. She turned aside and, crossing a bit of elastic, dry grass, climbed to the top of the stone wall and looked about her. Her heart throbbed with confidence, doubly grateful for the previous distrust. Her own lines came back to her; it was this that somehow, imperfectly, but somehow, she had put into words. It was still spring, a late New England spring, though the unseasonable warmth of the day made it seem summer. The landscape bore the coloring of autumn rather than that of the earlier year. The trees were red and brown and yellow in their incipient leafage. Now and then, among the sere fields, there was a streak of vivid green, or a mound of rich brown, freshly turned earth; but for the most part they were bare. Here and there was the crimson of a new maple; in the distance were the reds and brown of new, not old, life. Only the birds sang as they never sing in autumn, a burst of clear, joyous anticipation—the trill of the meadowlark, the "sweet, sweet, piercing sweet" of the flashing oriole, the call of the catbird, and the melody of the white-bosomed thrush. And here and there a fountain of white bloom showed itself amid the sombreness of the fields, a pear or cherry tree decked from head to foot in bridal white, like a bit of fleecy cloud dropped from the floating masses above to the discouraged earth; along the wayside the white stars of the anemone, the wasteful profusion of the eyebright, and the sweet blue of the violet; and in solemn little clusters, the curled up fronds of the ferns, uttering a protest against longer imprisonment—let wind and sun look out! they would uncurl to-morrow! All these things set the barely blossomed branches, the barely clothed hillsides, at defiance. It was the beginning, not the end, the promise, not the regret—it was life, not death. Summer was afoot, not winter.

It was worth a longer walk, that half hour on the hillside; for it restored, in a measure, her sense of enjoyment, and substituted for the burden of defeat the exultation of expression, however faulty and however limited. But like other moods, this one was temporary; and as she retraced her steps and turned into the village street, she felt again the lassitude which follows the extinction of hope and the inexorable narrowing of the horizon which she had fancied extended.

It was usual for her at this hour to stop at the tavern for the mail which might be ready there, and herself take it to the post-office. In midsummer this mail was quite an important item, but at this time of year it amounted to little; nevertheless, she followed what had become the custom. She found one of the daughters of the house in the throes of composition.

"Oh, Lucyet," she exclaimed, "you don't say that's you! I want this to go to-night the worst way. Ain't you early?"

"Yes, I guess I am," said Lucyet, rather wearily.

"If you'll set on the piazzer and wait, I'll finish up in just a minute. You see we had to get dinner for two gentlemen as came down to go fishin' to-morrer, and it sorter put me back. I wish you'd wait."

"Well, I guess I can wait a few minutes," said Lucyet, the line between her personal and her official capacity being sometimes a difficult one to maintain rigidly. She seated herself on the piazza, not observing that she was just outside of the window of the room within which the two fishermen were smoking and talking in a desultory fashion. Later their voices fell idly on her ear, speaking a language she only half understood, blending with the few lazy sounds of the afternoon. The conversation was really extremely desultory, being chiefly maintained by the younger man of the two, who lounged on the sofa of unoriental luxury with a thorough-going perversion of the maker's plan,—his head being where his feet ought to have been and his feet hanging over the portion originally intended for the back of his head. The other man wore the frown of absorption as, a pencil in his hand, he worried through some pages of manuscript.

"Oh, I say," observed the idler, "ain't you 'most through slaughtering the innocents? I want to take that walk."

"I told you half an hour ago that if I could have a few uninterrupted minutes I'd be with you," answered the other man, without looking up. "They haven't fallen in my way yet."

"It's pity that moves me to speech," rejoined the first speaker, rising and sauntering to the window,—not that one outside of which Lucyet was sitting,—"pity for those young souls throbbing with the consciousness of power who may have forgotten to enclose a stamp for return. I feel when I interrupt you as if I were holding back the remorseless wheel of fate."

His companion allowed this speculative remark to pass without reply. The idler sauntered back to the table.

"What'll you bet, now, before you go any further, that it'll go into the waste-basket?"

"Stamped and addressed envelope enclosed," observed the patient editor, absently.

"Well, what odds will you give me of its being not necessarily devoid of literary merit, but unfitted for the special uses of your magazine?"

The other was still silent as he laid aside another page.

"Half the time," continued the idler, "to look at you, you wouldn't believe that you speak the truth when you express your thanks for the pleasure of reading their manuscripts. It would seem that that, too, was simulated."

The older man picked up a soft felt hat and threw it across the room at his companion, without taking his eyes from the page.

"Oh, well," went on the other, "I can read the newspaper. I can read what is printed, while you're reading what ought to be. Of course you and I know the things are never the same."

Picking up the paper, he resumed, approximately, his former attitude, and applied himself to its columns for a few moments of silence. Outside Lucyet sat quietly, her head resting against the white wooden wall of the house; and the editor made a mark or two.

"Now this is what the public want to know," resumed the idler, with a gratuitous air of having been pressed for his opinion. "You editors have a ridiculous way of talking about the public—"

"It strikes me that it is not I who have been making myself ridiculous talking about anything."

"The public! You just tell the great innocent public that you are giving them the sort of thing they like, and half the time they believe you, and half the time they don't. Now this man"—and he tapped the "Chronicle"—"knows an editor's business."

"Which is more than you do," interpolated the goaded man.

"'The frame for William Brown's new house is up. William may be trusted to finish as well as he has begun,'" read the idler, imperturbably. "'Miss Sophie Brown is visiting friends in Albany. The boys will be glad to see her back.' 'Fruit of all kinds will be scarce, though berries will be abundant.'"

The older man stood up, his pencil in his mouth. "Confound you, Richards! Either you keep still or I go to my room and lock the door."

"Oh, I'll keep still," said Richards, as if it was the first time it had been suggested. Again there was a silence.

The letter must be to Ada's young man, who was doing a good business in cash registers, it took so long to write it. It was within five minutes of the time Lucyet should be at the office. She moved to leave the piazza, when a not loud exclamation from Richards fell on her ear with unusual distinctness.

"By Jove! I say, just listen to this."

The editor looked up threateningly, and went back to his work again without a word.

"No, but really—it's quite in your line. Listen."

Lucyet had moved forward a step or two, when she stood motionless. The words that floated through the window were her own. Richards had an unusually sweet voice, and he was reading in a way entirely different from that in which he had rattled off the "personals." There seemed a new sweetness in every syllable; the warmth of the hillside, the perfume of opening apple blossoms, breathed between the lines. He read slowly, and the words fell on the still air that seemed waiting breathless to hear them. When he finished, Lucyet was leaning against the side of the house, her hand on her heart, her eyes shining,—and the editor was looking at the reader.

"There," he concluded, "ain't there something of the 'blackbird's tune and the beanflower's boon' in that?"

"Copied, of course?" inquired the editor, briefly.

"No. 'Written for the Daily Chronicle,' and signed 'L.' Not bad, are they? Of course I don't know," Richards scoffed, "and the public wouldn't know if it read them, but you know—"

"Read 'em again."

A second time, with increased expression, half mischievous now in its fervor, the lines on Spring fell in musical tones from

Richards's lips. Still Lucyet stood breathless, her whole being thrilled with an impulse of exultant, inexpressible delight, listening as she had never listened before. It was as if she stood in the midst of a shining mist.

"She's got it in her, hasn't she?" Richards added, after a pause.

"Yes," said his companion, slowly. "She's got it in her fast enough;" and he returned to his page of manuscript. "Much good may it do her!" he added, with weary cynicism.

Richards laughed, and pulled a pack of cards out of his pocket. "I'll play solitaire," he said.

"Thank Heaven!" murmured the other, devoutly.

Ada arrived breathless. "Here 'tis," said she. "Did you think I was never comin'? You've got time enough; they ain't very prompt. There ain't anythin' the matter, is there?" she asked.

Lucyet took the letter mechanically. "No," she said, "there isn't anything the matter."

As she went swiftly toward the little post-office the rhythm of those lines was in her ears; the assured, incisive tones of that man's voice pulsed through her very soul. She was conscious of no hope for the future; she had no regret for the past; the present was a glory. In that moment Lucyet had taken a long, dizzying draught from the cup of success.

Hearts Unfortified

THE observation train wound its way in clumsy writhings along the bank of the river, upon which the afternoon light fell in modified brilliancy as the west kindled towards the sunset. But if the sheen and sparkle of the earlier day had passed into something more subdued and less exhilarating, the difference was made up in the shifting action and color that moved and glowed and flashed on, above and beside the soft clearness of the stream. The sunlight caught the turn of the wet oars and outlined the brown muscular backs of the young athletes who were pulling the narrow shells. The Yale blue spread itself in blocks and patches along the train, and the Harvard crimson burned in vivid stretches by its side, and all the blue and crimson seemed instinct with animation as they floated, quivered, and waved in the thrilled interest of hundreds of men and women who followed with eager eyes the knife-blades of boats cleaving the water in a quick, silent ripple of foam. The crowd of launches, tugs, yachts, and steamers pushed up the river, keeping their distance with difficulty, and from them as well as from the banks sounded the fluctuating yet unbroken cheers of encouragement and exhortation, rising and falling in rhythmic measure, guided by public-spirited enthusiasts, or breaking out in purely individual tribute to the grand chorus of partisanship. It had been a close start, and the furor of excitement had spent itself, somewhat, during the first seconds, and now made itself felt more like the quick heart-beats of restrained emotion as the issue seemed to grow less doubtful, though reaching now and then climaxes of renewed expression.

"Alas for advancing age!" sighed a woman into the ear of her neighbor, as their eyes followed the crews, but without that fevered intensity which marked some other glances.

"By all means," he answered. "But why, particularly, just now? I was beginning to fancy myself young under the stress of present circumstances."

"Because even if one continues to keep one's emotions creditably—effervescent—one loses early the single-minded glow of contest."

"A single-minded glow is a thing that should be retained, even at considerable cost."

"And what is worse yet, one grows critical about language," she continued calmly, "and gives free rein to a naturally unpleasant disposition under cover of a refined and sensitive taste."

Ellis Arnold smiled tolerantly.

"They are pretty sure to keep their lead now," he said. "The other boat is more than a length behind, and losing. They are not pulling badly, either," he added. "You were saying?"—and he turned towards her for the first time since the start.

She was a handsome blonde-haired woman, perfectly dressed, with the seal of distinction set upon features, figure, and expression.

"That was what I was saying," she replied, "that the ones that are behind are not pulling badly."

"More sphinx-like than ever," he murmured. "I perceive that you speak in parables."

Miss Normaine laughed a little. The conversation was decidedly intermittent. They dropped it entirely at times, and then took it up as if there had been no pause. It was after a brief silence that she went on: "But you and I can see both boats—the success, and the disappointment too. And we can't, for the life of us, help feeling that it's hard on those who have put forth all their strength for defeat."

"But it isn't so bad as if it were our boat that was behind," he said sensibly.

"Oh, no; of course not. But I maintain that it injures the *fine fleur* of enjoyment to remember that there are two participants in a contest."

"I suppose it is useless to expect you to be logical—"

"Quite. I know enough to be entirely sure I'd rather be picturesque."

"But let me assure you, that in desiring that there should be but one participant in a contest, you are striking at the very root of all successful athletic exhibitions."

She shrugged her shoulders a little.

"Oh, well, if you like to air your powers of irony at the expense of such painful literalness!"

"The exuberance of my style has been pruned down to literalness by the relentless shears of a cold world. With you, of course,"—but he was interrupted by the shouts of the crowd, as the winning boat neared the goal. The former enthusiasm had been the soft breathings of approval compared to this outbreak of the victorious. Flags, hats, handkerchiefs rose in the air, and the university cheer echoed, re-echoed, and began again.

Arnold cheered also, with an energy not to be deduced from his hitherto calm exterior, standing up on the seat and shouting with undivided attention; and Miss Normaine waved her silk handkerchief and laughed in response to the bursts of youthful joy from the seat in front of her.

"Oh, well," said Arnold, sitting down again, "sport is sport for both sides, whoever wins—or else it isn't sport at all."

"Ah, how many crimes have been committed in thy name!" murmured Miss Normaine.

"Katharine, I think you have turned sentimentalist."

"No, it's age, I tell you. I'm thinking more now of the accessories than I am of the race. That's a sure sign of age, to have time to notice the accessories."

Arnold nodded.

"There's compensation in it, though. If we lose a little of the drama of conflict on these occasions, we gain something in recognizing the style of presentation."

"Yes," and she glanced down at her niece, whose pretty eyes were making short work of the sunburned, broad-shouldered, smooth-faced, handsome boy, who was entirely willing to close the festivities of Commencement week subjected to the ravages of a grand, even if a hopeless, passion.

From her she looked out upon the now darkening river. There had been some delay before the train could begin to move back, and the summer twilight had fallen; for the race had been at the last available moment. Though it was far from quiet, the relief from the tension of the previous moments added to the placidity of the scene. The opposite banks were dim and shadowy, and the water was growing vague; there were lights on some of the craft; a star came out, and then another; there were no hard suggestions, no sordid reminders. It was a beautiful world, filled with happy people, united in a common healthy interest; the outlines of separation were softened into ambiguity and the differences veiled by good breeding.

"It is only a mimic struggle, after all," she said at last. "The stage is well set, and now that the curtain is down, there is no special bitterness at the way the play ended."

"There you exaggerate, as usual," he replied, "and of course in another direction from that in which you exaggerated last time."

"The pursuit of literature has made you not only precise but didactic," she observed.

"There is a good deal, if not of bitterness, of very real disappointment, and some depression."

"Which will be all gone long before the curtain goes up for the next performance."

"Ah, yes, to be sure; but nevertheless you underrate the disappointments of youth,—because they are not tragic you think they are not bitter,—you have always underrated them."

She met his eyes calmly, though he had spoken with a certain emphasis.

"We are talking in a circle," she replied. "That was what I said in the first place—that as we grow older we have more sympathy with defeat."

"You are incorrigible," he said, smiling; "you will accept neither consolation nor reproof."

"Life brings enough of both," she answered; "it does not need to be supplemented by one's friends."

The train was moving very slowly; people were laughing and talking gayly all about them; more lights had come out on the water, and a gentle breeze had suddenly sprung up.

"Just what do you mean by that, I wonder?" he said slowly.

"Not much," she answered lightly. "But I do mean," she added, as he looked away from her, "that, whether it be the consequence of the altruism of the day, or of advancing age, as I said at first, it has grown to be provokingly difficult to ignore those who lose more serious things than a college championship. Verestchagin and such people have spoiled history for us. Who cares who won a great battle now?—it is such a small thing to our consciousness compared to the number of people who were killed—and on one side as well as the other."

"Except, of course, where there is a great principle, not great possessions, at stake?"

"Yes," she assented, but somewhat doubtfully, "yes, of course."

"But it shows a terrible dearth of interest when we get down to principles."

"Yes," she said again, laughing. Meanwhile Miss Normaine's niece was pursuing her own ends with that directness which, though lacking the evasive subtlety of maturer years, is at once effective and commendable.

"It was nothing but a box of chocolate peppermints," she insisted. "I'd never be so reckless as to wager anything more without thinking it over. I have an allowance, and I'm obliged to be careful what I spend."

He looked her over with approval.

"You spend it well," he asserted.

"I have to," she returned, "or else boys like you would never look at me twice."

"I don't know about that." He spoke as one who, though convinced, is not a bigot.

"It's fortunate that I do," she replied decidedly. "I'm mortifyingly dependent on my clothes. There's my Aunt Katharine now,—she has an air in anything."

"I like you better than your aunt," he confessed.

"Of course you do. I've taken pains to have you. But it was just as much as ever that you looked at me twice last night."

"I was afraid of making you too conspicuous."

"A lot you were!" she retorted rudely. "Who was that girl you danced with?"

He smiled wearily.

"Tommy Renwick's cousin from the West."

"She is pretty."

"Very good goods."

"Is she as nice as Tommy?"

"No. There are not many girls as nearly right as Tommy."

"Except me."

"Well, perhaps, except you."

"But then, I'm not many."

"No, separate wrapper, only one in a box," he admitted handsomely.

Miss Normaine's niece had dark eyes, brown hair that curled in small inadvertent rings, and a rich warm complexion through which the crimson glowed in her round cheeks. She was so pretty that she ought to have been suppressed, and had a way of speaking that made her charming all over again.

"It was not chocolate peppermints, and you know quite well it wasn't," he said, with the finished boldness compatible with hair parted exactly in the middle and a wide experience. Miss Normaine's niece opened her eyes wide.

"What was it?"

"Nothing but your heart."

She considered the matter seriously.

"Was it really?"

"It was really."

"And I've lost," she pondered aloud.

"And you've lost."

She raised her eyes with a glance in which he could read perfect faith, glad acknowledgment, and entire surrender.

"Do you want me to keep telling you?" she demanded with adorable petulance.

"There is Henry Donald!" exclaimed Miss Normaine. "I didn't see him before. He has grown stout, hasn't he?"

"Yes, and bald."

"Isn't he young to be bald and stout too? Do tell me that he is," urged Miss Normaine with pathos. "He seems just out of college to me, and I don't like to think that I've lost all sense of proportion."

"Oh, no, you haven't," said Arnold, consolingly. "It's only he that has lost his. He doesn't take exercise enough. He's coming this way to speak to you. You had better think of something more flattering to say."

"I never thought Harry Donald would get stout and bald," went on Miss Normaine, to herself. "There was a period when I let my fancy play about him, most of the time too, but I never thought of that."

"Who's that man squeezing through the crowd to speak to Aunt Katharine?" asked Alice.

"That? Oh, that's one of the old boys."

"I can see that for myself."

"He's a Judge Donald of Wisconsin. He's pretty well on, but he's a Jim-dandy after-dinner speaker. Made a smooth speech at his class reunion."

"They still like to come to the race and things, don't they?"

"Oh, yes, and they're right into it all while they're here too."

Unhappily unconscious of the kindly feeling being extended to him from the bench in front, Judge Donald seated himself by Katharine, just as they drew slowly into the station.

"You haven't been on for some years, have you?" she asked him.

"No," he answered, "I've been busy."

"Oh, we know you've been busy," she interpolated, smiling.

"You're the same Katharine Normaine," he rejoined. "I thought you were, by the looks, and now I'm sure. You don't really know that I've ever had a case, but you make me feel that my name echoes through two worlds at the very least."

"And you are still Harry Donald, suspicious of the gifts that are tossed into your lap," and they both laughed.

"This is the man of the class," went on Judge Donald, turning to Ellis, who had taken a seat above them. "Your books have gotten out to Wisconsin, and that's fame enough for any man."

"Have they really?" said Arnold. "I supposed they only wrote notices of them in the papers."

"Oh, yes," murmured Miss Normaine. "Ellis has turned out clever,—one never knows."

"I guess they're good, too," went on Donald; "I tell 'em I used to think you wrote well in college."

"I thought I did, too," answered Arnold. "I don't believe we're either of us quite so sure I write well now."

They had delayed their steps to keep out of the crowd, for the people were leaving the train, some hurrying to catch other trains, some stopping to greet friends and acquaintances; there was a general rushing to and fro, the clamor of well-bred voices, the calling out of names in surprised accost, the frou-frou of gowns and the fragrance of flowers, in the bare and untidy station.

At last the party of which Miss Normaine was one left the car, and with the two men she made her way down the platform, through the midst of the hubbub, which waxed more insistent every moment.

"It is with a somewhat fevered anxiety that I am keeping my eye on Alice," she said.

"She is with a young man," said Judge Donald.

"That statement has not the merit of affording information. She has been with a young man ever since we left home."

"It isn't the same one, either," supplemented Arnold.

"It never is the same one," said Miss Normaine, somewhat impatiently. "I am under no obligation to look after or even differentiate the young men. I simply have to see that the child doesn't get lost with any one of them."

"She won't get lost with one," said Arnold, reassuringly, as they were separated by a cross-current of determined humanity. "She has three now, and they are all shaking hands at a terrible rate."

Judge Donald departed on a tour of investigation, and returned to say that there was no chance just at present of their getting away. It was a scene of confusion which only patience and time could elucidate. The omniscience of officials had given place to a less satisfactory if more human ignorance; last come was first served, and a seat in a train seemed by no means to insure transportation. It was as well to wait for a while outside as in; so with many others they strolled up and down, until their car should be more easily accessible.

"Alice is an example of the profound truths we have been enunciating, Ellis," said Miss Normaine. "She has an ardent admirer on the defeated crew. At one time I did not know but his devotion might shake her lifelong allegiance to the other university; but now that victory has fairly perched, you observe she has small thought for the bearers of captured banners. We were saying, Mr. Arnold and I," she explained to Donald, "that it is at our time of life that people begin to remember that when somebody beats, there is somebody else beaten."

Donald grew grave,—as grave as a man can be with the feathers of an unconscious girl tickling one ear and a fleeting chorus of the latest "catchy" song penetrating the other.

"Arnold and I can appreciate it better than you, I guess," he said, "because there have been times when we thought it highly probable we might get beaten ourselves."

"Highly," assented Arnold.

"But you, Miss Normaine, you've never had any difficulty in getting in on the first floor," went on the other. "You've quaffed the foam of the beaker and eaten the peach from the sunniest side of the wall right along—I'm quite sure of it just to look at you."

"The Scripture moveth us in sundry places," said Katharine, with a lightness that did not entirely veil something serious, "not to put too much faith in appearances. Even I am not above learning a lesson now and then."

He looked at her curiously.

"I'd like to know by what right you haven't changed more," he said.

"Did you expect to find me in ruins, after—let me see, how many years?" she laughed. "The hand of Time is heavy, but not necessarily obliterating. What has become of Alice?"

"She can't have gone far," said Arnold. "She was with us a moment ago."

"There she is with some of the rest of your party—I caught a glimpse of her just now," added Donald. "She's quite safe."

Alice stood talking with a girl of her own age and two or three undergraduates, on the outskirts of the crowd. One of the youths wore in his buttonhole the losing color, but he bore himself with a proud dignity that forbade casual condolences. Alice's eyes were bright, and her pretty laugh rippled forth with readily communicated mirth, while the very roses of her hat nodded with the spirit of unthinking gayety.

"There's the car that belongs to our fellows," said, half to himself, the person of sympathies alien to those of his present companions. "They must be about—yes, they're getting on," he added, as a car which had been propelled from a neighboring switch stopped at the farther end of the station. Alice's head turned with a swiftness of motion that set the roses vibrating as if a sudden breeze had ruffled their petals.

"The crew?" she asked.

"Yes," assented the young man.

She turned more definitely towards him, away from the rest of the group, whose attention was called in another direction.

"Will you do something for me, Mr. Francis?"

"Why, of course."

Alice had not anticipated refusal, and her directions were prompt and lucid.

"Please go into that car and ask Mr. Herbert to come out to the platform, at the other end, to speak to me. There isn't much time to lose, so please be quick."

As he lifted his hat and moved away, she joined in the conversation of the others, which seemed to be largely metaphorical.

"So he got it that time," one of the young men was explaining, "where Katy wore the beads."

"Well, it served him quite right," said Alice, with the generosity of ignorance. Her whole attention was apparently given to the matter in hand, but she was standing so that she could see the somewhat vague vestibule of the brilliant but curtained car.

"Oh, yes, but it wasn't on the tintype that the other fellow should have been there at all."

"No, to be sure, but that made it all the better," said Alice's friend, with sympathetic vision.

"Why, there's Eugene Herbert!" exclaimed Alice. "I really must go and tell him that he pulled beautifully, if he didn't win, and comforting things like that! Don't go off without me."

Before comment could be framed upon their lips, she had left her companions and was slipping quickly down the platform.

"She knows him very well," said the other girl; "she'll be back in a minute."

"She must have sharp eyes," said another of the group, as he looked after her. But too many people were about for fixed attention to be bestowed upon a single figure. There was but one light under the roof of that part of the station where a young man was standing, looking rather sulkily up and down. Alice was a little breathless with her rapid walk when she reached him.

"I thought Francis was giving me a song and dance," he said, as he grasped the hand she held out.

"No, I sent him," she explained hurriedly. "And I wanted to say—"
She paused an instant as she looked up at him.

He was serious, and wore a look of fatigue, in spite of the superb physical health of his whole appearance. The light fell across her face under the dark brim of her hat, and touched its beauty into something vividly apart from the shadows and sordidness of the place, yet paler than its sunlit brilliancy.

"I wanted to say," she went on bravely, "that I've changed my mind. At least, I didn't really have any mind at all. And if you still want me to—" she paused again, but something in his eyes reassured her—"I will—I'd really *like* to, you know, and *please* be quiet, there isn't but a minute to say it in—and I'd never have told you—at least not for years and *years*—if you had won the race. Now let go of my hand—there are *hundreds* of people all about—and you can come and see me to-morrow."

It was all over in a moment. She had snatched her hand away, and was speeding back with a clear-eyed look of conscious rectitude, and he had responded to the exhortations of divers occupants of the car, backed by a disinterested brakeman, and stepped aboard.

"Oh, well, there's another race next year," he said to somebody who spoke to him as he sat down in the end seat. It was early for such optimism, and they thought Herbert had a disgustingly cheerful temperament.

Alice returned just as Miss Normaine and Arnold came up, and they all went back together, collecting the rest of the party as they went to their train. It was a vivacious progress along the homeward route. Pæans of victory and the flash of Roman candles filled the air. At one time, when some particular demonstration was absorbing the attention of the men, Miss Normaine found her niece at her side.

"Aunt Katharine, you know I've always adored you," she said, with a repose of manner that disguised a trifle of apprehension.

"Yes, I know, Alice, but I really can't promise to take you anywhere to-morrow. I—"

"I don't want you to—I only want to confide in you."

"Oh, dear, what have you been doing now?"

"I think," replied Alice, while the chorus of sound about them swelled almost to sublimity, "that I've been getting engaged—to Eugene Herbert, you know."

"Only to Eugene Herbert," breathed Miss Normaine. "I'm glad it occurred to you to mention it. But why didn't you say so before?"

"It didn't—it wasn't—before," said Alice, faltering an instant under the calmly judicial eye of her aunt. "You see," she went on quickly, "it was because they lost the race. It wouldn't have been at all—not anyway for a long time,"—and again her mental glance swept the vista of the years she had mentioned to Herbert himself,—"if it hadn't been for that; but I couldn't let him go back without either the race or—or me," she concluded ingenuously.

Arnold had been talking with a man of his own age, and hearing things that were very pleasant to hear about his latest work, and yet, as he leaned back in his chair and looked across at Katharine Normaine, whose own expression was a little pensive, he sighed. It was a great deal—he told himself it was nearly everything—to have what he had now in the line of effort which he loved and had chosen. It was not so good as the work itself, of course, but the recognition was grateful. And as his eyes dwelt again upon the distinction of Miss Normaine's profile, with the knot of blonde hair at the back of her well-held head, he sighed again, as he rose and went over to her. She looked up at him, and her eyes were not quite so calm as usual.

"I am sitting," she said, "among the ruins."

"Indeed?" he said. "Is there room upon a fallen column or a broken plinth for me?"

"Oh, yes," she answered, "but it is not for a successful man like you, whose name is upon the public lips, to gaze with me upon demolished theories."

"I have taken my time in gazing upon them before now," he observed.

"Everybody is talking about your book," she said.

"Oh, no, only a very few people. But about your theories—which of them has proved itself unable to bear the weight of experience?"

"You may remember I dwelt somewhat at length upon the indifference of happy youth to the stings of outrageous fortune when supported by some one else?"

"I remember. I regard it as the lesson for the day."

"It's early to mention it, but I am obliged to give you the evidence of my error—honor demands it—and Alice will not mind, even if she sees fit to contradict it to-morrow;" and she told him what had just been told her.

He smiled as she concluded her statement, and she, meeting his glance in all seriousness, broke down into a moment's laughter.

"'She does not know anything but that her side is beating,'" he quoted meditatively.

"I thought my generosity in confession might at least forestall sarcasm," she said severely.

"It ought to do so," he admitted.

There was a moment's pause.

"Has youth itself changed with the times, I wonder?" he speculated. "Certainly you did not sympathize overmuch with defeat at Alice's age."

She did not answer, and she was looking away from him through the glass, beyond which the darkness was pierced now and then by a shaft of illumination. The pensiveness that had rested on her face, when he had looked across the car at her, had deepened almost into sadness.

"And now," he went on, "you have called me successful—which shuts me out from your more mature sympathy."

Still she did not answer. He bent a little nearer to her.

"Believe me, Katharine," he said, "my success is not so very intoxicating after all. I need sympathy of a certain kind as much as I did twenty years ago."

She glanced at him.

"Is that all you want?" she asked with a swift smile.

"No," he returned boldly; and she looked away again, out into the darkness through which they were rushing.

"I had hoped," he went on, "that my so-called success might be something to offer you after all this time—something you would care for—and now I find that your ideals are all reversed. I have not won much, but I have won a little, and you tell me to-day that it is only extreme youth that cares for the winners."

"And that I have found out that I was mistaken." Her voice was low, but quite clear. "Have I not told you that, too?"

"And about experience of life making us care the more for those who fail in everything?"—he waited a moment. "You have not mentioned that that was a mistake also. I wish you'd stop looking out of that confounded window," he added irritably, "and look at me. Heaven knows I've failed in some things!"

She laughed a little at his tone, but she did not follow his suggestion.

"Oh, no," she said, "you have succeeded."

"And that means—what?"

"I told you I was sitting among the ruins of my theories," she said, while a faint color, which he saw with sudden pleasure, rose in her cheek.

"That adverse theory—has that gone too?"

"I have had enough of theories," she declared softly. "What I really care for is success."

Her Neighbors' Landmark

THE sun had not quite disappeared behind the horizon, though the days no longer extended themselves into the long, murmurous twilight of summer; instead, the evening fell with a certain definiteness, precursor of the still later year.

On the step of the door that led directly into the living-room of his rambling house sat Reuben Granger, an old man, bent with laborious seasons, and not untouched by rheumatism. The wrinkles on his face were many and curiously intertwined; his weather-beaten straw hat seemed to supply any festal deficiency indicated by the shirt-sleeves; and his dim eyes blinked with shrewdness upon the dusty road, along which, at intervals, a belated wagon passed, clattering. His days of usefulness were not over, but he had reached the age when one is willing to spend more time looking on. He had always been tired at this hour of the day, but it was only of late that fatigue had had a certain numbing effect, which disinclined him to think of the tasks of tomorrow. He came to this period of repose rather earlier nowadays, and after less sturdy labor—somehow, a great deal of the sturdy labor got itself done without him; and there was an acquiescence in even this dispensation perceptible in the fall of his knotted hands and the tranquil gaze of his faded eyes.

About a dozen yards beyond him, on the doorstep leading directly into the living-room of a house which joined the other, midway between two windows (the union marked by a third doorway unused and boarded up, around whose stone was the growth of decades), sat Stephen Granger. His weather-beaten straw hat shaded eyes dim also, but still keen; and a network of curious wrinkles wandered over his tanned and sun-dried skin. Upon his features, too, dwelt that look of patient tolerance that is not indifference, that only the "wise years" can bring; and on his face as well as his brother's certain lines about the puckered mouth went far to contradict it. If one saw only one of the old men, there was nothing grim in the spectacle—that of a weary farmer looking out upon the highroad from the shelter of his own doorway; but the sight of them both together took on suddenly a forbidding air, a suggestion of sullenness, of dogged resolution; they were so precisely alike, and they sat so near one another on thresholds of the same long, low building, and they seemed so unconscious the one of the other. It was impossible not to believe the unconsciousness wilful and deliberate. A heavily freighted and loose-jointed wagon rattled noisily but slowly along the road.

"Howaryer?" called out one of its occupants.

"'Are yer?" returned Stephen Granger.

Reuben had opened his mouth to speak, but closed it in silence, while he gazed straight before him, unseeing, apparently, and unheeding. The leisurely driver checked his horse, which responded instantly to the welcome indication. Behind him in the wagon two calves looked somewhat perplexedly forth, their mild eyes, with but slightly accentuated curiosity, surveying the Grangers and the landscape from the durance of the cart.

"Been tradin'?" asked Stephen.

"Wal, yes, I have," answered the other, with that lingering intonation that seems to modify even the most unconditional assent.

"Got a good bargain?"

"Wal, so-so."

"Many folks down to the store this evenin'?"

"Wal, considerable."

"Ain't any news?"

"Not any as I know on."

Stephen nodded his acceptance of this state of things. The other nodded, too. There was a pause.

"G'long," said the trader, as if he would have said it before if he had thought of it. But the horse had taken but a few steps when another voice greeted him.

"Howaryer, Monroe?" said Reuben Granger.

"Whoa," said Monroe. "Howaryer?"

"Been down to the Centre?" asked Reuben.

"Yare."

"Got some calves in there, I see."

"Wal, yes; been doin' some tradin'."

Reuben nodded. "Ain't any news, I take it?"

"None in partickler." Another exchange of nods followed.

"G'long," said Monroe, after a short silence, during which the calves looked more bored than usual. But the shaky wheels had made but a few revolutions before the owner of the wagon reined in again.

"Say," he called back, twisting himself around and resting his hand on the bar that confined the calves. "They've took down the shed back of the meetin'-house. Said 'twas fallin' to pieces. Might 'a' come down on the heads of the hosses. Goin' to put up a new one." Then, as his steed recommenced its modest substitute for a trot, unseen of the Grangers he permitted himself an undemonstrative chuckle. "They can sorter divide that piece of news between 'em," he said to his companion, who had been the silent auditor of the conversation. A moment of indecision on the part of the Grangers had given him time to make this observation, but it was not concluded when Reuben's cracked voice sang out cheerfully, "Ye don't say!" A slight contraction passed over Stephen's face. Much as he would have liked to mark the bit of information for his own, now that it had been appropriated by another, he gave no further sign. The noise of the wagon died along the road, and still Reuben and Stephen Granger sat gazing straight before them at the hill which faced them from the other side of the way, at the foot of which the darkness was falling fast. By and by a lamp was lighted in one half of the house, and a moment later there was a flash through the window of the other, and slowly and stiffly the two old men rose and went inside, each closing his door behind him.

"Them's the Granger twins," had said the owner of the calves in answer to his companion's question as soon as they were out of hearing. "Yes, they be sort of odd. Don't have nothin' to say to one another, and they've lived next door to each other ever since they haven't lived *with* each other. It's goin' on thirty years since they've spoke. Yes, they do look alike—I don't see no partickler difference myself, and it would make it kinder awk'ard if they expected folks to know which one he's talkin' to. But they don't. They're kinder sensible about that. They're real sensible 'bout some things," he added tolerantly. "Oh, they was powerful fond of each other at first—twins, y' know. They was always together, and when each of 'em set up housekeepin', nothin' would do for it but they should jine their houses and live side by side—they knew enough not to live together, seein' as how, though they was twins, their wives wasn't. So they took and added on to the old homestead, and each of 'em took an end. Wal, I dunno how it began—no, it wasn't their wives—it don't seem hardly human natur', but it wasn't their wives." The speaker sighed a little. He was commonly supposed to have gained more experience than felicity through matrimony. "I've heard it said that it was hoss-reddish that begun it. You see, they used to eat together, and Stephen he used to like a little hoss-reddish along with his victuals in the spring, and Reuben, he said 't was a pizen weed. But there! you can never tell; they're both of 'em just as sot as—as erysipelas; and when that's so, somethin' or other is sure to come. I know for a fact that Reuben always wanted a taste of molasses in his beans, and Stephen couldn't abide anythin' but vinegar. So, bymeby, they took to havin' their meals separate. You know it ain't in human natur' to see other folks puttin' things in their mouths that don't taste good to yours, and keep still about it."

His companion admitted the truth of this statement.

"Sometimes I think," went on Monroe, musingly, "that if they'd begun by eatin' separate they might have got along, 'cause it's only His saints that the Lord has made pleasant-tempered enough to stand bein' pestered with three meals a day, unless they're busy enough not to have time to think about anythin' but swallerin'. Hayin'-time most men is kinder pleasant 'bout their food—so long 's it's ready. Wal, however it was, after they eat separate there was other things. There was the weather. They always read the weather signs different. And each of 'em had that way of speakin' 'bout the weather as if it was a little contrivance of his own, and he was the only person who could give a hint how 'twas run, or had any natural means of findin' out if 'twas hot, or cold, or middlin', 'less he took hold and told 'em. It's a powerful tryin' sort of way, and finally it come so that, if Reuben said we was in for a wet spell, Stephen 'd start right off and begin to mow his medder grass, and if Stephen 'lowed there was a sharp thunder-shower comin' up, inside of ten minutes, Reuben'd go and git his waterin'-pot and water every blamed thing he had in his garden. I dunno when it was they stopped speakin', but that was about all there was to it—little things like that. They didn't either of 'em have any children; sometimes I've thought if they had, the kids might sort of brought 'em together—they couldn't have kep' 'em apart without they moved away, and of course they wouldn't either of 'em give in to the other enough to move away from the old farm. Then their wives died 'bout a year from each other. They kep' kind o' friendly to the last, but they couldn't stir their husbands no more'n if they was safes—it seems, sometimes, as if husbands and wives was sort o' too near one another, when it comes to movin', to git any kind of a purchase. When Reuben's wife died, folks said they'd have to git reconciled now; and when Stephen's died, there didn't seem anythin' else for 'em to do; but folks didn't know 'em. Stephen went up country where his wife come from and brought home a little gal, that was her niece, to keep house for him; and then what did Reuben do but go down to Zoar, where *his* wife come from, and git her half-sister—both of 'em young, scart little things, and no kin to one another—and *they* can't do nothin' even if they wanted to. Bad-tempered? Wal, no. I wouldn't say the Granger twins was bad-tempered;" and the biographer dexterously removed a fly from his horse's patient back. "They're sot, of course, but they ain't what they used to be—I guess it's been a sort of discipline to 'em—livin' next door and never takin' no kind of notice. They're pleasant folks to have dealin's with, and I've had both of 'em ask me if I cal'lated it was goin' to rain, when I've been goin' by—different times, o' course—but it 'most knocked the wind out of me when they done it, 'stead of givin' me p'inters. Yes, you never can speak to 'em both at once, 'cause the other one never hears if ye do; but there! it ain't much trouble to say a thing over twice—most of us say it more'n that 'fore we can git it 'tended to; and," he added, as he leaned forward and dropped the whip into its socket preparatory to turning into his own yard, "most of us hears it more'n once."

"Monroe," called a voice from the porch, "did you bring them calves?"

"Yare," said Monroe.

"I told you if you stopped to bring 'em, you wouldn't be home till after dark."

"Wal?"

"I told you 't would be dark and you'd be late to supper."

"Wal?" and Monroe took down the end of the wagon, and persuaded out the calves.

The person who was Monroe's companion and the recipient of his confidences was a young woman who was an inmate of his house for the present month of September.

Confident and somewhat audacious in her conduct of life, Cynthia Gardner had felt that this September existence lacked a motive for energy before it brought her into contact with the Granger twins.

"They are so interesting," she said to Monroe, a day or two later.

"Wal, I guess they be," answered Monroe, amiably. The quality of being interesting did not assume to his vision the proportions it presented to Cynthia Gardner's, but he saw no reason to deny its existence. Cynthia cast a backward glance from the wagon as she spoke, and saw Reuben slowly and stiffly gathering up dry stalks in his garden, while Stephen propped up the declining side of a water-butt in his adjoining domain, one man's back carefully turned to the other.

She walked back from the Centre, and stopped to talk with the twins in a casual manner. But no careful inadvertence drew them, at this or any later time when their social relations had become firmly established, into a triangular conversation. They greeted her with cordiality, responded to her advances, talked to her with the tolerant and humorous shrewdness that lurked in their dim eyes, but it was always one at a time. If, with disarming naïveté, she appealed to Stephen, Reuben turned into a graven image; and if she chaffed with Reuben, Stephen became as one who having eyes seeth not, and having ears heareth not. But she persisted with a zeal which, if not according to knowledge, was the result of a firm belief in the possibility of a final adjustment of differences. She did not know, herself, what led her into such earnestness,—a caprice, or the lingering pathos of two lonely, barren lives.

Monroe watched her proceedings with tolerant kindliness. It was not his business to discourage her. He knew what it was to be discouraged, and he felt that there was quite enough discouragement going about in life without his adding to it.

"I tell you they would like to be reconciled, Mr. Monroe," said Cynthia. "They don't know they would like it, but they would."

"Wal, mebbe they would. They're gittin' to be old men. And when you git along as far as that, you don't, perhaps, worry so much about *bein'* reconciled, but neither does it seem as worth while *not* to. There's a good deal that's sort of instructive about gittin' old," he ruminated.

"It's very lonely for them both, I think;" and Cynthia's voice fell into the ready accents of youthful pity.

"Their quarrel's been kinder comp'ny for 'em," suggested Monroe.

"It's overstayed its time," asserted Cynthia.

"Mebbe," answered Monroe.

The crisis—for Cynthia had been looking for a crisis—came, after all, unexpectedly. She had been for the mail, and as she drove the amenable horse over the homeward road she strained her eyes to read the last page of an unusually absorbing letter, for it was again sundown, and the Granger twins again sat in their doorways There was a decided chill in the air, this late afternoon. The old men, though they were sturdy still, had put on their coats, and from behind them the comfortable glow of two stove doors promised a later hour of warmth and comfort. Their aspect was more melancholy than usual, whether it were that the bleakness of winter seemed pressing close upon the bleakness of lonely age, or that there was an added weariness in the droop of the thin shoulders and the fixed eyes—it was certain that the picture had gained a shadow of depression.

For once, Cynthia was not thinking of them as she drew near. The reins were loose in her hand, and as she bent to catch the waning light, an open newspaper, which she had laid carelessly on the seat beside her, was lifted by a transient gust of wind and tossed almost over her horse's head. No horse, of whatever serenity, can be thus treated without resentment. He jerked the reins from her heedless hands, made a sharp turn to avoid the white, wavering, inconsequent thing at his feet, a wheel caught in a neighboring boulder, and Cynthia was spilled out just in front of the Granger house and midway between the twins. In a common impulse of fright the two old men started to their feet. For an instant they paused to judge of the situation, but it was no time for fine distinctions. The accident had, to all appearances, happened as near one as the other, and meanwhile a young and pretty woman lay unsuccored upon the ground. It became a point of honor to yield nothing to an ignored companion. As speedily as their years allowed, Stephen and Reuben marched to the rescue. The horse, meanwhile, had dragged the overturned wagon but a few yards, and had stopped of his own reasonable accord. As Cynthia raised herself rather confusedly and quite convinced that she was killed, her first impression was that the angels were older than she had fancied and looked very much like the Granger twins. But in a few seconds her balance of mind was restored, she realized that while there was life there was hope, and that for the first time in her experience the eyes of Reuben and Stephen were fixed solicitously upon a common object, that each of them had stretched out to her a helping hand, and that two voices with precisely the same anxious intonation were saying,—

"Be ye hurt?"

It was a solemn moment, but Cynthia Gardner was of the stuff that recognizes opportunity. She laid a hand upon each rugged arm, and steadied herself between them; she perceived that they trembled under her touch, and she felt that the instant in which they stood side by side was dramatic.

"I declare, 'twas too bad," said Reuben.

"'Twas too bad," said Stephen.

"Is the horse all right?" asked Cynthia, feebly.

"Yes, Johnny Allen got him," said Stephen.

"Johnny Allen came along," said Reuben, as if Stephen had not spoken, "and he's got him."

"I can walk," she said, with not unconscious pathos, "if you will walk with me, but I must go in and rest a moment;" and the three moved slowly straight forward.

A few steps brought them to the point at which they must turn aside to reach either entrance. Before them rose the old boarded-up, dismal doorway, weather-beaten, stained, repellent as bitterness. There was another fateful pause. Cynthia felt the quiver that ran through the frames of the old men as for the first time in long years they stood side by side before the doorway about which as children they had played, and through which as boys they had rushed together. In Cynthia's drooping head plans were rapidly forming themselves, but she had time to be thankful that she did not know which was Reuben and which was Stephen—it saved her the anxiety of decision; instinctively she turned to the right, a small brown hand clutching impartially either rough and shabby sleeve.

The man on her right swerved in an impulse of desertion, but her grasp did not relax.

"Is the judgment of Solomon to be pronounced!" she said to herself, half hysterically, for her nerves were a little shaken.

"Oh, I hope I sha'n't faint!" she exclaimed aloud.

Beneath Reuben's rustic exterior beat the American heart that cannot desert an elegant female in distress. He followed the inclination of the other two to Stephen's door, and in another never-to-be-forgotten moment he stepped inside his brother's house.

Stephen's deceased wife's niece was so overcome by the spectacle that she retained barely enough presence of mind to drag forward a wooden chair upon which Cynthia sank in a condition evidently bordering upon syncope. It was a critical moment; she must not give the intruder an opportunity to escape. She knew the intruder by that impulse of desertion, and she clung the tighter to his arm when she murmured pitifully, "If you could get me some water, Mr. Granger."

Stephen hastened towards the kitchen pump—the sight of Reuben in his side of the house, after thirty years, set old chords vibrating with a suddenness that threatened to snap some disused string, and his perceptions were not as clear as usual. He seized the dipper, filled it, and looked about him.

"Where's the tumbler, Jenny?" he called impatiently.

"It's right there," answered the girl, with the explicitness of agitation.

"Whar?" he demanded with asperity.

"Settin' on the side—right back of the molasses jug."

"Molasses jug!" he exclaimed. "Nice place for the molasses jug!"

"We was goin' to have baked beans for supper," said the trembling Jenny, feeling that it was best to be tentative about even a trifling matter within the area of this convulsion, "and you always want it handy."

It was a simple statement, but it laid a finger upon the past and upon the future. Cynthia, through her half-closed eyes, saw one old man with disturbed features, standing with his hand upon her chair, while another old man shuffled toward her with a glass of water, which spilled a little in his shaking hand as he came across the humble kitchen. Most inadequate dramatic elements, yet they held the tragedy of nearly a lifetime, and the comedy, though more evident, was cast by it in the shade, and she neither laughed nor cried.

Within a few moments more she was on her homeward way, a trifling break in the harness tied up with twine, and Johnny Allen in the seat beside her as guard of honor.

The next evening the people, driving home from the Centre, were saved from some active demonstration only by the repression of the New England temperament. Some of them even, after driving past, invented an errand to drive back again, so as to make sure. For the Granger twins sat side by side in front of the disused doorway, and their straw hats were turned sociably towards one another, now and then, as they exchanged a syllable or two, and there was a mild luminousness of pleasure in the recesses of their pale-blue eyes. The evening darkened fast into night. The plaintive half-chirp, half-whistle of a tree-toad fell in monotonous repetition upon the ear.

"Hear them little fellers!" said Stephen, ruminantly. "I reckon they think it's goin' to rain."

"Yare," said Reuben. "And," he went on, pushing back his straw hat and looking up into the sky, "I wouldn't wonder if they was right."

"Mostly are," said Stephen.

The End

www.ingramcontent.com/pod-product-compliance
Lightning Source LLC
Chambersburg PA
CBHW071353310526
45790CB00017B/378